"Bruce has a remarkable ability to examine today's important management issues and provide useful and 'hands on' tools to help every organization improve their leadership effectiveness. I really appreciate the unique insight in this book and will be able to use this to tackle this important challenge with our changing workforce."

Jon Morrison, President, WABCO, Americas

"Once again Bruce has his finger on the pulse beat... As with his previous works addressing generational differences within the workplace, the reader finds him/herself nodding in recognition of the behaviors characterized by Gen Zers. Bruce goes beyond the commentary by providing practical guidance on how employers can work with their young talents to help them develop the soft skills they will require in order to reach their full potential"

Jack Dwyer, VP Human Resources and Administration,
ASSA ABLOY, Inc.

"Well researched, practical and immensely readable, *Bridging the Soft Skills Gap* is destined to be a go-to book for any leader charged with managing during this turbulent changing of the employee guard."

Joni Thomas Doolin, CEO, TDn2k; Founder, People Report

Traditional rules don't apply in appealing to and engaging our extremely talented younger generation. This book is a valuable and practical resource for any manager who wants to effectively manage and motivate this important and ever-growing part of our workforce."

Andy Ajello, Senior Vice President of Diabetes & Obesity Sales, Novo Nordisk, Inc.

"As companies like ours develop new solutions in a rapidly transforming industry, it is critical that we identify, recruit and engage new talent that can help lead these transformations. Bruce provides a critical tool in this step by step training guide."

Raymond R. Ferrell - EVP General Counsel and Corporate
Secretary, Dex Media, Inc.

"This book reflects authentic thought leadership and will be of great value to all executives who are smart enough to buy the book!"

Daniel Butler, Senior Advisor, National Retail Federation; President, Maple Point Consulting

"Bruce Tulgan has done it again. He has not only well framed the issue of the soft skills gap, but has also given today's managers practical advice for dealing with it."

Hank Harris, President and Chief Executive Officer, FMI Corporation

"Teaching today's young talent basic soft skills can be a magnificent legacy for seasoned pros. This book is a must-read for managers in any industry, and it is especially relevant in the service sector where soft skills are the face of our business."

Sharon McPherson, Director of Training & Development,
On The Border Restaurants

"Bruce's book is such a timely and relevant read for managers. As always, he masterfully lays out the research as to what makes Gen Zers unique, why we should be excited to have them, and the most effective performance development strategies to motivate and bring out the best in them. The best part of this book is the hundreds of practical and adaptable lesson plans he provides to develop basic, yet vital interpersonal skills to help an early career professional become your strongest contributor."

Kristen Storey, Organizational Learning Director, Learning &
Professional Development, University of Michigan

"HOW you conduct yourself and get the work done will always trump technical skills. This book distills the HOW in a way that can truly transform performance. It is a wealth of information and on-point in speaking to an issue we need to harness in the workplace quickly, and should be mandatory reading for every manager/leader out there!"

Melissa Feck, Vice President, Human Resources,
Health Care Association of New York State

"Bruce Tulgan's book provides great insight, ideas and resources for a manager leading the new college graduates in the workforce. Adjusting to a regular schedule and leaving the freedom of college and youth is a challenge for many - they lack many soft skills. Bruce provides specifics to help the leader guide the new employee to learn key skills in the context of the work which helps them be successful without losing their desire to be unique."

Sue Hiser, Program Director, Leadership Development,
Ohio Health

"Bruce Tulgan has done it again. *Bridging the Soft Skills Gap* doesn't just describe the challenges I see every day with my talented young team - it provides real tools for their development. Businesses and their valued young employees will benefit from these resources and reap long-term rewards."

Janet Kyle Altman, Marketing Principal,
Kaufman Rossin

"If you want to learn how to teach, inspire and lead today's young talent, read as Bruce magically mixes actual life examples with solid leadership principles. This book will give you complete knowledge of what you need to know to lead today."

Doug Sterbenz, EVP & COO Westar Energy (Retired); Present to Win,
National Speaker and Leadership Coach

"Many managers lament that Millennials lack soft skills like professionalism or followership but then struggle with how to address the gap. In his now well established style, Bruce Tulgan's latest book offers detailed, practical training lesson plans for each of a dozen soft skills. "

Alan Krezco, "The Artist formerly known as" Executive Vice
President and General Counsel (retired), The Hartford

"After reading this book, I just keep thinking, 'It all makes sense now!' Incredible insight into understanding the next generation of talent in today's workforce. This book has forced me to think about how to restructure on-boarding and training efforts that will result in more successful and productive employees and teams."

Sheri Petrie, Training & Coaching Consultant, Mid-Atlantic
Permanente Medical Group

"This remarkable book is a must have for any manager with young talent to lead. With extensive scripts and step-by-step lesson plans to improve what Tulgan calls the 'missing basics,' it provides everything a manager needs to turn a mediocre younger worker into a truly valued, key player."

Deborah Orlowski, Ph.D., Senior Learning Specialist, Learning and
Professional Development, University of Michigan.

"This is one of the best books I have ever read when it comes to teaching "soft skills" to a group of young employees in the workplace. To bridge the gap between Gen Z and their supervisors, managers, leaders, and executives and create a collaborative workforce both groups are provided with specific skills sets through exercises and concepts. The book is a must read for those who want to increase their productivity and workplace morale."

Steve Hanamura, President, Hanamura Consulting, inc.; Consultant, speaker and author

Bridging the Soft Skills Gap

HOW TO TEACH THE MISSING BASICS TO TODAY'S YOUNG TALENT

BRUCE TULGAN

JOSSEY-BASS
A Wiley Imprint
www.josseybass.com

Published by John Wiley & Sons, Inc., Hoboken, New Jersey.
Published simultaneously in Canada.

For general information on our other products and services or for technical support, please contact our Customer Care Department within the United States at (800) 762-2974, outside the United States at (317) 572-3993 or fax (317) 572-4002.

Wiley publishes in a variety of print and electronic formats and by print-on-demand. Some material included with standard print versions of this book may not be included in e-books or in print-on-demand. If this book refers to media such as a CD or DVD that is not included in the version you purchased, you may download this material at http://booksupport.wiley.com. For more information about Wiley products, visit www.wiley.com.

Library of Congress Cataloging-in-Publication Data:

Tulgan, Bruce, author.
  Bridging the soft skills gap : how to teach the missing basics to today's young talent / Bruce Tulgan.
       pages cm
  Includes index.
   ISBN 978-1-118-72564-1 (cloth); ISBN 9781119138150 (ePDF); ISBN 9781119138167(ePub)
   1. Soft skills. 2. Generation Y--Employment. 3. Business etiquette. 4. Personnel management. I. Title.
   HF5381.T757 2015
   658.3'124   dc23

2015016765

Printed in the United States of America

10 9 8 7 6 5 4 3 2 1

This book is dedicated to my beloved agent, the great genius

—Susan Rabiner

Contents

Acknowledgments

This book is the product of more than twenty years of ongoing research on young people in the workplace. At this point, all told, hundreds of thousands of individuals have contributed to our surveys, interviews, and focus groups since we first began our workplace research in 1993. First and foremost, I always thank everyone who has participated in this research over the years.

Thanks also to the very many business leaders who bring me in to learn from and help your managers facing real challenges every day in the real world. To the hundreds of thousands who have attended my keynote addresses and seminars: thanks for listening, for laughing, for sharing the wisdom of your experience, for pushing me with the really tough questions, for your kindness, and for teaching me. My greatest intellectual debt is to the managers who have participated in our seminars—I've learned so much from helping them wrestle with their very real management problems in the real world. Special thanks to those managers whose real stories appear in this book; I've mixed up the ancillary details to help keep the stories anonymous.

Welcome to Dr. Bennett Graff, our new chief of operations at RainmakerThinking. Thank you for your confidence in this enterprise and the excellent contributions you are making every day to our mission and our business. We are going to do great things together, Bennett.

To our very dear old friends and my interim management team, business partners Chris Glowacki and Kristin Campbell and their entire family to the furthest extent of consanguinity, but especially Lily, Albert, Herbie, and Stella: Thank you for your friendship and your family and your contributions to this enterprise. I am very grateful. We love you all, every one.

To Susan Ingraham, my longtime executive assistant (and one of the most reliable, considerate, even-tempered, and good-hearted people I have ever known): Thank you so much for everything you do, Susan. I honestly don't know what I would do without you. You have my undying gratitude and loyalty.

To Liz Richards, who has been serving at RainmakerThinking for less than a year at this writing (but has already proven herself among the very best of her very young generation): Thank you, Liz, for your everyday professionalism, critical thinking, and followership. We are very grateful.

Now, to the publisher and the editors:

To everyone at Wiley and Jossey-Bass: Thanks to every one of you who has put your faith and good thinking and hard work into the books we have done together, especially this one.

Karen Murphy, my editor on THE 27 CHALLENGES MANAGERS FACE, and my editor on this book until the late stages, has moved on in her career, but not before helping me conceive and re-conceive this book a number of times. Thanks to you, Karen, for all of your help along the way.

My brand new editor, the very talented and skilled Judy Howarth, has adopted me and this project in the late stages. She did so with kindness and conviction, and I have no doubt that her excellent work makes this book very much better. I am extremely grateful.

Then I always come to the great, great, great Susan Rabiner, to whom this book is dedicated. Susan is not only a world-class literary agent for me and also for my wife, Debby. Susan has become a true, dear, beloved friend and absolutely one of our very most favorite people in the world. When this book was going through draft after draft—when I was struggling to zero in on the issues that were truly at stake and the research that was truly most relevant— Susan demonstrated why she is considered one of the most brilliant minds in non-fiction publishing. Since we first met in the late 1990s, I have not written a book that Susan has not influenced profoundly. But this book is dedicated to Susan because her guidance and support in this effort was beyond even her usual heroics. It is not an overstatement to say that Susan Rabiner is simply the smartest and the best editorial mind in non-fiction publishing. She and her husband, the late genius Al Fortunato, wrote the book about writing and publishing non-fiction, *Thinking Like Your Editor: How to Write Great Serious Nonfiction—and Get It Published*. Susan is nearly 100 percent responsible for my success as a writer. How can I thank Susan enough?

My family and friends are the anchors of meaning in my life. First, thanks to my parents, Henry Tulgan and Norma Propp Tulgan, for raising me as well as you did. You are both among my very closest friends to this day, and I treasure the time we spend together. I neglected to visit my beloved parents for several months because I was so under the gun finishing this book in time. I would be ashamed for not visiting more except that the whole time, true to form, they insisted, "Don't come visit until you finish your book. We'll see you when you finish." What I owe to my parents could fill much more than one book, but it definitely includes my work ethic!

Thanks also to the rest of my beloved family: My parents-in-law, Julie and Paul Applegate; my nieces and nephews (from oldest to youngest): Elisa, Joseph, Perry, Erin, Frances, and Eli; my sister, Ronna, and my brother, Jim; my sister in-law, Tanya, and my brothers in-law, Shan and Tom. I love every one of you very, very much.

I always add a special extra thanks to my niece, Frances, because I have always thought of her as if she were my own child.

Finally, I always reserve my last and most profound thanks for my wife, Debby Applegate. For many years now, Debby and I have worked side-by-side, writing. For me, to be writing in her company is an honor and an inspiration. Among her many impressive credentials, Debby won the 2007 Pulitzer Prize for her biography of Henry Ward Beecher! While I have made my way through this manuscript, Debby has been hard at work on what is likely to be yet another of the great American biographies of this century. This one is about a now largely forgotten figure of the 1920s—Polly Adler. Just wait. You're going to be bowled over by it. It's hard to believe that, by the date this book is published, it will be thirty years since our first date in September of 1985. We've been together ever since. There is nothing—absolutely nothing—I have done since the day I met Debby that has not been profoundly influenced by her. Debby is my constant adviser, my toughest critic, my closest collaborator, the love of my life, my best friend, my smartest friend, my partner in all things, half of my soul, owner of my heart, and the person without whom I would cease to be.

PART ONE

THE SOFT SKILLS GAP

Prologue

Meet the Newest New Young Workforce

Today's newest new young workforce has so much to offer—new technical skills, new ideas, new perspectives, new energy. Yet, too many of them are held back—and driving the grownups crazy—because of their weak soft skills.

Managers tell us every day in our research some version of what one middle-aged manager in a pharmaceutical company told me: "When I was young and inexperienced, I may have been naïve or immature, but I knew enough to wear a tie, make eye contact, say 'please' and 'thank you' and 'yes, sir' and 'yes, ma'am,' and when to shut up and keep my head down and do the grunt work without having to be told over and over again."

Indeed, the incidence and insistence of managers complaining about the soft skills of their new young workers has risen steadily year after year since we began tracking it in the mid-1990s, when Generation Xers were the "New Dogs" on the scene. Specifically, what issues do managers complain about most? Here's what managers most often say:

"They are unprofessional."
"They have no self-awareness."
"They don't take personal responsibility or hold themselves accountable.
"They need an attitude adjustment."
"Their work habits are terrible."
"Their people skills are terrible."
"They don't know how to think, learn, and communicate without checking a device."

"They don't think critically."

"They don't know how to problem solve, make decisions, and plan."

"They have problems deferring to authority."

"They don't appreciate context and see where they fit in."

"They have no sense of self-sacrifice for the greater good."

"What ever happened to citizenship, service, and teamwork?"

There is a growing gap between the expectations of employers and the reality of how today's new young talent is showing up in the workplace. Today's young stars may well show up with the latest and greatest skills and methods. Indeed, many of them seem to have developed almost "superpowers" in their chosen areas of interest and focus. They are often masters of the newfangled. What they are missing—way too often and more and more—is the old-fashioned basics, what many refer to as "the soft skills."

What do young people have to say about the widely perceived widening soft-skills gap? Mostly, they say, "That's so true about my friends and me!" or else "Seriously?!" and then, either way, "So what?!"

To that, I usually respond, "Well, it drives the grown-ups crazy and it's holding you back. If you were to radically improve on these soft skills, it would give you a huge strategic advantage in your career." The good news is that this is almost always enough explanation to capture their attention and interest in improving.

An executive in a major financial services institution recently told me about a recruiting interview with a very strong job candidate just about to graduate from college: "In the middle of my pitch about the long-term rewards of making a career in a company like ours, this young man starts laughing out loud. I mean actually laughing, just for a second. Then he quickly regained his composure. He was very apologetic. But what he said really struck me. He said, 'Sir, you must realize that it's very hard for someone in my position to have any kind of faith in those long-term promises. I mean: Didn't we just barely avoid having another depression a couple of years ago? It's not that I don't trust YOU. It's just that I don't trust the future.'"

The executive said, "What really struck me was that, of course, he's exactly right. There is so much complexity and uncertainty in the external risk factors. Why in the world would anyone trust the long-term promises of an institution like ours?"

What do business leaders and managers say when I tell them how they can lead their new young talent through the growing soft-skills gap? Often the first response is something like this response from a long-time partner in a large accounting/consulting firm: "This should NOT be our problem to solve! Shouldn't they have already learned all these old-fashioned basics from their parents? Or in kindergarten? Or at least in high school or college? Or graduate school for that matter? Certainly by the time they come to work as an associate at this firm, they should know how to get themselves to work on time and behave properly. Am I supposed to teach them how to cross the street, too?"

That comment brings to mind an aggressive public service campaign sponsored mainly by Yale University, here in New Haven, Connecticut, where we live. The City and the University have sponsored signs all over town, as well as other public education resources, spelling out the basics of safe pedestrian behavior. This was in part a response to the ubiquitous traffic hazard of Yale students jaywalking while staring down at their hand-held devices. In other words, some of the smartest kids in the world today—the cream of the crop, the future doctors, scientists, accountants, engineers, professors, and leaders in every industry—needed an aggressive public education program in order to learn how to cross the street. As one official told me: "They have all the latest tools and tricks, but I guess they are somewhat lacking in a lot of the old tricks. What's really interesting is that the program works. They are actually getting much better at crossing the street."

Here's what I tell my clients: If you employ young people nowadays, then the soft-skills gap is your problem. That's the bad news. So here's some good news: You can bridge the soft-skills gap, and doing so will give you a huge strategic advantage when it comes to hiring the best young talent, bringing them on board and up-to-speed faster, better performance management, improved relationships, and greater retention rates among the best young talent.

The CEO of a biotech company in Silicon Valley was hosting a half-dozen employees at his weekly "lunch with the CEO." Making conversation with the twenty-two-year-old brand new employee to his left, he asked, "Did you just graduate this past May or were you working somewhere else prior to joining us?" She said she had just graduated. The CEO asked, "That's great. Congratulations. We are glad to have you." And then he asked, "Where did you go to school? What did you study?" The new young employee answered. The CEO continued, "Excellent. Did you do any part-time work while you were in school?" To this, the young woman replied, "That's enough about me, alright? What about you? What's your story?" The CEO chuckled as he told me this story. He told me, "I wanted to say, 'My story? I'm your boss's boss's boss's boss. That's my story. But instead I just told her my story.'" He concluded, "It just took me aback, being so young and so junior in her role, her lack of inhibition in talking to the CEO of her new employer."

For years, I've used the military as my "ace in the hole" when making the business case that organizations can and should invest in bridging the soft-skills gap. I would typically point to the Marines' Boot Camp, for example, and say, "The Marines can take an ordinary young person and turn him or her into a United States Marine in just thirteen weeks, and together these young Marines make up the most effective fighting force in the history of the world." Of course, most organizations don't have the resources (or the inclination) to run the equivalent of their own boot camp. (Some do, by the way, and it works like a charm. But those organizations are few and far between.)

The really good news is that you don't have to put your young employees through the equivalent of a boot camp in order to have a huge impact on their soft skills. In fact, we've collected hundreds of case studies, best practices, and teaching methods from organizations and individual managers who have systematically helped their new young employees radically improve their soft skills. There are many, many ways you can help them build up one soft skill at a time and thereby make them much more effective and successful employees, co-workers, and future leaders.

Chapter 1

The Soft Skills Gap

You are very careful in your recruiting, selection, and hiring process and, yet, it is getting harder and harder to figure out which young job candidates to hire. Should you hire the promising new graduate with impressive, freshly minted credentials indicating valuable technical skills, even though he seems like he might be yet another new graduate lacking in some of those elusive, yet critical "soft skills"?

It seems like more and more of your young new hires are not working out. They make very little effort to "fit in." Does every single one of them expect to be treated like a "special case"? They often don't seem to appreciate that they are entering a pre-existing scene; joining an organization with its own mission, history, structure, rules, and culture; integrating with a group that has its own established dynamic; and engaging with individuals, each of whom has his or her own story and many of whom have been part of this scene in this organization for years on end or longer.

Too often they say the wrong things at the wrong times and they fail to ask a lot of the questions they should be asking. Heck, they often can't even get to work on time. Anyway, they spend half the workday on their devices, instead of focusing on the work. That really comes through in customer service scores, along with other complaints about young front-line service personnel. Sometimes, their lack of interpersonal skills leads to misunderstandings and even conflicts on the team.

Most of them seem to have one foot out the door from the day they arrive, all the while asking for more of something—or more of everything. Even the young superstars nowadays don't seem to come in early, stay late, work through meals and weekends and holidays, bend over backward, and jump through hoops like the young superstars of yesteryear did.

If you are like most managers with employees in their late teens and twenties, then you no doubt have first-hand experience with a very serious management challenge that has been growing especially fast in recent years. There is an ever-widening "Soft Skills Gap" in the workforce, especially among the newest new young workforce.

I use the term "soft skills" because most people understand the term is used, in contrast to "hard skills" which are technical, to encompass a wide range of non-technical skills ranging from "self-awareness" to "people skills" to "problem solving" to "teamwork."

These skills may be less tangible and harder to define and measure than many of the "hard skills," but they are absolutely critical to the success or failure of any individual in the workplace. The problem is that these old-fashioned basics—professionalism, critical thinking, and followership—are out of fashion and are too rarely spoken of nowadays. Today's young talent is not being indoctrinated in these old-fashioned basics either at home or in school. Usually, by the time they get to the workplace, employers figure it is too late to focus on them. Certainly, most managers think it is neither their place, nor do they have the time or resources or know-how to deal with the soft skills gap in their newest, youngest employees. So the soft skills gap continues to grow, hiding in plain sight, despite the fact that it costs organizations a fortune every day.

I've asked tens of thousands of managers: "How much do these so-called 'soft skills' matter?" The answer is nearly universal: Soft skills matter a lot. The cliché is that people are hired because of their hard skills but people are fired because of their soft skills.

When employees have significant gaps in their soft skills, there are significant negative consequences: Potentially good hires are overlooked. Good hires go bad. Bad hires go worse. Misunderstandings abound. People become distracted. Productivity goes down. Mistakes are made. Customer service suffers. Workplace conflicts occur more frequently. Good people leave when they might have otherwise stayed longer.

It robs so many young employees of greater success and causes so many managers so much aggravation and so many unnecessary costs. The soft skills gap is not a household term like the technical skill gap, but it should be, because its impact is monumental.

Like the technical skill gap, the soft skills gap in the workforce has been developing slowly for decades. But the soft skills gap runs across the entire workforce—among workers with technical skills that are in great demand, every bit as much as workers without technical skills. What is more, the soft skills gap has grown much worse in recent years.

Are today's young employees really so much worse when it comes to soft skills than those of previous generations?

At the corporate headquarters of a very old and very large consumer products conglomerate, summer interns are sometimes permitted to attend certain high-level meetings, mostly as a learning experience, but also to run errands and assist with clerical tasks during the meetings. One such intern was visibly annoyed when she was asked by her manager to dress in "business casual attire, at least" on days when she would be attending such meetings. After, "ignoring that suggestion entirely," the intern came to one such meeting "very casually dressed" and then spent most of the meeting texting on her hand-held device. When her manager whispered quietly to ask her to please stop texting during the meeting, the intern responded in an exasperated tone, "Actually, no." The manager whispered back with incredulity: "'No'?" At which point, the intern explained, "I'm texting with my dad . . . about this meeting. So, it's fine. My dad works here!" As it turned out, she was giving a blow-by-blow account of the meeting in progress to her father, who was himself a longtime executive in the company, and had arranged the internship with the company for his daughter.

The Soft Skills Gap: Growing Steadily from Gen X to Gen Y to Gen Z

Since 1993, I've been tracking generational change in the workplace and its impact on organizations, especially the impact on supervisory relationships. I started out as a frustrated young lawyer seeking to understand why the older, more experienced lawyers were so annoyed by those of my generation, Generation X (born 1965 to 1977). I quickly realized that it wasn't just the older, more experienced people at my firm who were annoyed with Gen Xers. It was nearly everybody older and more experienced in workplaces of all shapes and sizes.

That's when I started conducting in-depth interviews with young people and their managers, the original research that led to my first book, *Managing Generation X.* I formed a company to continue that research, and we've been conducting that interview research for decades now, tracking the ever-emerging, ever-"newer" new young workforce. By the late 1990s, we started tracking the first wave of the great Millennial cohort, what we refer to as "Generation Y" (born 1978 to 1989). At this point, we've been tracking the second wave Millennials, whom we call "Generation Z" (born 1990 to 1999), for nearly a decade now, since they first entered the workforce as teenagers in part-time jobs. Gen Zers are the newest "New Dogs" arriving in your workplace, part of the global youth tide rising now and for the foreseeable future.

I've interviewed tens of thousands of young workers (hundreds of thousands of interviewees in total) in just about every industry—health care, professional services, restaurants, retail, research, finance, aerospace, software, manufacturing, the public sector, even nonprofits—you name it. Based on two decades of research, I can report that the overwhelming data points to a steady diminution in the soft skills of young people in the workplace from Gen X to Gen Y to Gen Z. Today's young workers are increasingly likely to have significant notable weaknesses in one or several key soft skills.

Why is that?

Some partners at a forensic accounting firm told me of their latest young associate "case study." This first-year associate, a recent top graduate of a top school, was cutting-edge in his knowledge of a new set of tools and techniques for mining and analyzing data buried within evidentiary documents obtained during pre-litigation discovery. One of the partners said, "This kid had done some projects in school using this new approach and his technical knowledge in this area far surpassed anyone else in the firm. But he kept running into roadblocks because his communication made him seem so immature. At first, he couldn't get anybody to listen to him. Once we got him going on introducing the new process, I know it sounds petty, but he kept saying 'like, like, like' every other word, and he could barely look people in the eye or string three words together without saying 'like.'" In short, "His inability speak in a way that seemed even remotely professional was just rubbing people the wrong way, especially in meetings, though it wasn't very much better when he was working with people individually." One of the other partners explained, "We had to send him to a class." One of the other partners added, "It took a lot more than one class."

Something Much Larger Is Going on Here: The Post-Boomer Generational Shift

Of course, the older, more experienced people are always more or less annoyed by the attitudes and behavior of each successive new young generation. New young employees are, by definition, always younger and less experienced and, therefore, lacking in the corresponding maturity and patience. As they step into the adult world with youthful energy and enthusiasm, young workers often clash with their older colleagues. That's always part of the story. But there is something much bigger going on here.

On a macro level, Generation Z represents a tipping point in the post-Boomer generational shift transforming the workforce. With older (first-wave) Boomers now retiring in droves, they are taking with them the last vestiges of the old-fashioned work ethic. By 2020, more than 80 percent of the workforce will be post-Boomer—dominated in numbers, norms, and values by Generations X, Y, and Z. Generation Z will be greater than 20 percent of the North American and European workforce (and a much greater percentage in younger parts of the world, especially South Asia, Sub-Saharan Africa, and South America).

Much of why Generation Z seems like a new species from another planet is really just an accident of history. They just happen to be the generation to come of age in the 2010s, during an era of profound change and uncertainty driven by a confluence of epic historical forces.

GLOBALIZATION

Generation Z will be the first truly global generation—connecting and traveling to work across borders in every direction and combination. Unlike any other generation in history, Gen Z can look forward to a lifetime of interdependency and competition with a rising global youth tide from every corner of this ever-flattening world.

TECHNOLOGY

The pace of technological advance today is unprecedented. Information. Computing. Communication. Transportation. Commerce. Entertainment. Food. Medicine. War. In every aspect of life, anything can become obsolete any time—possibilities appear and disappear swiftly, radically, and often without warning.

A very savvy and experienced restaurant general manager, who employs more than a dozen teens and early twenty-somethings, shared this with me: "Schedule adherence is always an issue among new young employees, but it's getting much worse. More and more, we are having a terrible time with young waiters, kitchen support, and cleaners disappearing for 'breaks' in the middle of their shifts, not to mention calling out 'sick' too often, coming in late, and leaving before shifts are over." To make matters worse, it seems that whenever confronted about their timeliness by a manager, the young employees responded by pushing back. The general manager said, "They would always have an excuse and they'd be almost indignant about it. Every one of them is a 'special case.'" She reports: When his manager told him he was taking too many breaks, one young waiter told his manager, "You have to understand. I have ADD so I am going to need some help staying focused." Reprimanded about coming in late and leaving early, a young prep chef pushed back, "I'm home schooled, so I'm not really used to following a set schedule." When confronted about regular last-minute absences, a young cleaner explained, "Sometimes, I just don't feel up to working."

INSTITUTIONAL INSECURITY

Gen Zers were small children on 9/11/01 and young teenagers when the economy collapsed in 2008. Theirs is a world threatened by terrorism and environmental cataclysm; in which the economy fluctuates wildly from boom to bust; governments sometimes shut down or run out of money; great companies conquer or fail or merge or continually downsize, restructure, and reengineer. Institutions in every domain have been forced into a constant state of flux just in order to survive and succeed in this constantly changing world. Gen Zers know enough to know that they can't rely on institutions to be the anchors of their success and security.

THE INFORMATION ENVIRONMENT

Gen Zers are the first true "digital natives." They learned how to think, learn, and communicate in a never-ending ocean of information. Theirs is an information environment defined by wireless Internet ubiquity, wholesale technology integration, infinite content, and immediacy. From a dangerously young age, their infinite access to information and ideas and perspectives—unlimited words, images, and sounds—is completely without precedent.

HUMAN DIVERSITY

In every dimension, the world is becoming more diverse and more integrated. Generation Z will be the most diverse workforce in history, by far. That's true in terms of geographical point of origin, ethnic heritage, ability/disability, age, language, lifestyle preference, sexual orientation, color, size, and every other way of categorizing people. For one thing, the Generation Z workforce will include a global mix like never before. Equally important, Gen Zers see every single individual, with his or her own combination of background, traits, and characteristics, as his or her own unique diversity story. They value difference, uniqueness, and customization, most of all their own.

At the same time, Generation Z has been also been shaped by two very important micro-trends.

Helicopter-Parenting on Steroids. By the late 1990s, the Boomer-esque self-esteem–based "everyone gets a trophy" style parenting was morphing anew. The parents of these second-wave Millennials are mostly Gen Xers, who have had fewer children and typically have children at a later age than Boomers did. Xer parents have taken helicopter parenting to a whole new level. As one Gen Xer parent told me, "I don't want to make my kid just feel like a winner no matter what happens. I want to do everything I can to set him up with every possible advantage to make sure he has a big head start in the real world so he can win for real." Parents (and contingent authority figures) are so engaged in supervising and supporting children's every move, validating differences, excusing (or medicating) their weaknesses, and setting them up with every material advantage possible. In China, where there are so many only children due to the longstanding "single child policy," a similar trend in child rearing has yielded a phenomenon referred to by many as "Little Emperor Syndrome."

Gen Zers grew up spending most of their time ensconced in their own highly customized safety zones—the private comfort of protection and resources provided by responsible adults who are always supposed to be looking out for them. Gen Zers have been insulated and scheduled and supervised and supported to a degree that no children or young adults have ever have been before. It's been decades since children were told to "go outside and play." Even school no longer functions—as it used to—as a robust quasi-public sphere for children to "scrimmage" real-life social interaction. More Gen Zers per capita, by far, have been home-schooled than any generation since the rise of public schooling. Meanwhile, parental involvement in the classroom is more pervasive than ever before.

Gen Zers have grown accustomed to being treated almost as customers/users of services and products provided by authority figures in institutions, both in schools and in extracurricular activities, not to mention in their not infrequent experiences as actual customers.

As a result of all of this, relationship boundaries with authority figures are rather blurry for Gen Zers. They expect authority figures to be always in their corner, to set them up for success, and to be of service. They are often startled when authority figures see it otherwise.

In an aerospace company that hires hundreds of new young engineers every year, engineering group managers have been reporting that entry-level engineers quickly become frustrated and bored with repetitive tasks and narrow recurring responsibilities—so bored, in fact, that they are playing video games on their hand-held devices while working. The problem, of course, is that the work of entry-level engineers—like so much entry-level work—involves a lot of repetitive tasks and narrow recurring responsibilities. One of the engineering group managers said, "If we don't actively keep them engaged in the work, they get distracted, and then they slow down and they also start making more mistakes." Another group manager responded, "What are we supposed to do? I found it frustrating and boring when I had to do it, too. The work is the work. Should we have the older, more experienced engineers do all the grunt work so these first- and second-year engineers can do all the interesting work just so they will stay engaged? They are simply not qualified yet to do the more interesting work."

Virtual Reality. It's not just that they are always looking down at their hand-held devices. Gen Zers are always totally plugged in to an endless stream of content and in continuous dialogue—through social media–based chatting and sharing and gaming—with peers (and practical strangers), however far away (or near) they might be. They are forever mixing and matching and manipulating from an infinite array of sources to create and then project back out into the world their own ever-changing personal montage of information, knowledge, meaning, and selfhood.

They try on personas virtually. Social media makes it easy to experiment with extreme versions of one persona or another and more or less (or much more) crass means of expression.

Gen Zers are perfectly accustomed to feeling worldly and ambitious and successful by engaging virtually in an incredibly malleable reality, where the stakes can seem all important one moment, until the game is lost and reset with the push of a button.

In a nutshell, Generation Z—East, West, North, and South—might be seen as a rising global youth-tide of "Little Emperors" who have been told their whole lives that "all styles are equally valid" and try to "fit in" with each other, in a never-ending digital dance, by projecting their uniquely diverse persona(s) in their own highly customized virtual peer ecosystem.

Trying to make the adjustment to "fitting in" in the very real, truly high-stakes, mostly adult world of the workplace is a whole new game for them. And it's not really their kind of game. They are less inclined to try to "fit in" at work, and more inclined to try to make this "whole work thing" fit in with them.

Gen Zers Are the Ultimate Non-Conformists in an Age of Non-Comformism

If you think about it, soft skills are mostly about "fitting in"—making an effort to conform one's attitude and behavior to established standards of conduct—in order to engage and work together effectively with others in a shared enterprise. Here's the thing: Gen Zers are the ultimate non-conformists in an age of non-conformism.

For some time now, the pendulum of the zeitgeist has been swinging—more or less—away from conformism. Non-conformism is the belief that it is better for individuals to be unique and emphasize their individual differences from the group; conformism is the belief that it is better for individuals to subordinate their individual differences and adopt the normative/dominant attitudes and behaviors accepted by the group in order to "fit in." Of course, in any era, there are conformists and outliers, regardless of the zeitgeist. But the pendulum does swing one way or the other. Think of the relative conformism of the 1950s—when so many were trying to assimilate and come together after the global upheaval of World War II and its aftermath. The revolutionary non-conformity of the 1960s yanked the pendulum in the other direction, and it's been swinging that way ever since. There have been ebbs in the swing—notably in the middle 1980s and the years immediately following 9/11. Still, the pendulum has kept swinging away from conformism and toward a broad cultural relativism—for many good reasons.

It is unfortunate that cultural relativism has been widely misunderstood and is often misappropriated—in a classic case of "reductio ad absurdum"—by those who wish to argue that no expectations of conformity to any norms of conduct are legitimate. This is the kind of thinking that leads to the wishful notion that "all styles are equally valid."

The problem with that notion should be obvious: If everybody has his own style and some styles are mutually exclusive, then how are we all supposed to get along and work together in a shared enterprise? Try to imagine a communication system whereby everybody speaks his own language. Or picture a style of greeting strangers by punching them in the nose. These suggestions are ridiculous.

Yet, there are, in fact, many different ways to greet a stranger appropriately, depending on the community—or the time period—in which you live: Some people would bow. Others would shake hands. Some would hug. Others kiss on both cheeks. More and more people are bumping fists these days, partly due to the rise in awareness of especially pernicious contagious germs. Social norms are indeed highly variable depending on context: manners and etiquette, appropriate attire, hair styles, good grammar, even the very meaning of words in the same language. When I was working in Ireland in the 1980s, I asked a woman for a "ride" home. It turns out I should have asked for a "lift." "Ride" meant something very different in Ireland from its most common meaning in the United States. Perhaps nowadays asking someone for a "ride" in Ireland would be less shocking, with so much more shared global media. To wit, social norms also change over time.

It is easy to see why cultural relativism is so important to understand. It provides much of the intellectual underpinning behind some very important long-term cultural/social trends away from oppressively hierarchical systems and one-size-fits-all rules. Strict hierarchy and one-size-fits-all rules are extremely limiting. By design, they prescribe and proscribe the behavior of those who wish to belong. They constrain individual expression, creativity, and innovation. They exclude those outside the norm or unwilling to conform. Sometimes, they exclude people for very bad reasons, sometimes even with malice, as in, "No Irish Need Apply," a sign common in U.S. workplaces in the middle to late 19th Century. Cultural relativism teaches us that differences in norms and values are not an indication of moral failure. There may be many different ways to think about or do things that are equally legitimate, on some fundamental level, even if they might be more or less appropriate in one culture versus another. Plus, being open to people with differing norms and values can open valuable new opportunities and possibilities. Still, none of this means that "all styles are equally valid."

What it really means is that a style that may be appropriate in one time and place may not be appropriate in another. Any cultural anthropologist will tell you, the way to get along in a different culture is to adjust your attitude and behavior to what is appropriate in that place and time. That doesn't mean you have to compromise your values or integrity or abandon your "true self." It just means, if you want to develop good relationships with others and be effective, you have to be adaptable.

Dress codes offer a simple example. I often say, "If you don't want to wear a uniform, you shouldn't become a police officer, a firefighter, or a soldier." Uniforms function to help police, firefighters, and soldiers to identify each other in a crowd; signal to outsiders the special role of those in uniform; provide important information such as name and rank; and have built-in equipment for doing the job. Uniforms can make a lot of sense in some jobs. So where do you draw the line? What about suits and ties for men? Skirts and jackets for women? When I was a young associate at a Wall Street law firm in early 1990s, there was a serious broo-ha-ha among the young associates over women lawyers being required to wear skirts instead of pants. In the 1990s! The Gen X lawyers had a mini-revolt in favor of women being able to wear pantsuits. What rebels!

Some standards of conduct are more burdensome than others. Some are arbitrary, exclusionary, constraining, and worth resisting. Others are necessary, efficacious, and worth some inconvenience. How does one tell the difference? This question holds the key to bridging the soft skills gap with today's young talent.

The bottom line is this: You simply cannot have a functional workplace where everybody makes his or her own rules of conduct. Imagine an organization in which some employees support the mission, but others support the opposite mission. Where nobody agrees about who is in charge. Where people come and go whenever they feel like it. Where some people wear pantsuits and others wear bathing suits. Where people only work on the tasks and responsibilities they enjoy, insist on doing everything their own way, and only work with the people they like. Where meetings are held with no particular agenda and people are encouraged to blurt out whatever pops into their heads. Where people may or may not return each other's calls and emails. And so on.

Sometimes, conforming makes a lot of sense. Consider the essential soft skills such as the elements of professionalism, critical thinking, and followership. These are old-fashioned basics for a reason: They are time-tested best practices. They work.

Nobody needs Gen Zers to give up their uniqueness as individuals, their overall non-conformism, or adopt too many arbitrary, exclusionary, or overly constraining standards. But most managers would very much like Gen Zers to make some reasonable adaptations—to adjust at least some of their attitudes and behaviors to the realities of the adult workplace.

The Soft Skills Gap: The Missing Basics in Today's Young Talent

The problem is that Gen Zers are neither accustomed nor inclined to conform their attitudes and behavior for an institution or an authority figure (especially a non-parental authority figure).

Yes: They apply for the job. They accept the job. They might be excited about the job. They might want your approval. They usually are very keen to succeed. They definitely want the paycheck. Nonetheless, they usually do not realize just how much "just doing their own thing" makes their attitudes and behavior maladaptive in the real world of the workplace.

Most of them have no concept of the incredible power of the old-fashioned basics. They simply cannot fathom how much mastering the soft skills could increase their value as employees—not just right now, but for the remainder of their careers. Even if they do understand the value, most Gen Zers have no idea where to begin. They are usually just not that familiar with the old-fashioned basics—certainly they have very little experience. And like any skill, if one does not practice, one simply cannot master the essential soft skills.

Let's go back to the "ur" conundrum of the soft skills gap: The promising new graduate with impressive freshly minted credentials—especially in-demand technical skills—who is nonetheless lacking in soft skills. If you interviewed a new young worker like this one privately, as I do all the time in my research, she would probably start looking down at her hand-held device and say something like this: "I have, like, the hard skills they need? So they, like, shouldn't care so much about the soft skills. So I come in a little late or leave a little early or blow off the occasional meeting?? So what?! They should just, like, tell me what they need me to do?? Give me, like, the resources I need?? And I'll, like, get the job done?? Why do they keep, like, insisting I do everything their way?? Their way, like, makes no sense?? My way is, like, so much easier?? And I'm, like, not afraid to say so!"

This young person is in a real quandary. It is a quandary shared by so many young workers, not to mention their co-workers and managers, everywhere I go. Today's newest young people in the workplace have so much to offer. Yet too many of them are adding less value and undermining their own credibility because of their weakness in a whole bunch of old-fashioned basics.

What are the soft skills that young people are missing nowadays that the grown-ups really miss the most? There are so many of them. I've boiled them down to some key behaviors in three old-fashioned categories:

1. Professionalism,

2. Critical Thinking, and

3. Followership.

Let's take a closer look.

1. OLD-FASHIONED "PROFESSIONALISM"

Why don't young people today hold themselves to a higher standard when it comes to their attitude, work habits, and people skills?

Just like those of previous generations, Gen Zers' first real job usually coincides with their first real taste of adult freedom and autonomy. They embrace the freedom and autonomy of young adulthood, but often resist the attendant responsibility, discipline, and consistency. Why do they not, like those of previous generations, quickly realize that young adults need to make the adjustment to the grown-up world?

There are five reasons:

First, most Gen Zers are coming to you straight from school. If they have the most in-demand technical skills, then they are probably coming from college or university; maybe graduate school. That means they've probably become quite accustomed to a very luxurious form of pretend adulthood. I'm not blaming the institutions, but think for a moment about the college/university lifestyle from which your young employees come to you: Room and board are not only covered, but also arranged conveniently in close proximity to campus. College students are surrounded by their peers all the time, and often with intimate friends. College students have access to the resources of a major institution, but their only responsibilities are those of a valued customer. They have the support and services of staff, administration, and faculty, but their social status is determined by where they fit in with their peer group. Their "job" is a privilege for which someone else is paying (even if it is paid for by student loans, the tremendous cost of all this is deferred).

In exchange for all of this, one could make a strong argument that very little is required or expected of most young college/university students. Of course, there is substantial coursework. Still, they have very little supervision and a great deal of latitude in all manner of their personal habits and conduct. How many college students come to work for you who have been in the habit of staying up too late hanging out with their friends? Skipping too many classes? Doing their work at the last minute . . . or not at all? Then expecting to receive an inflated grade? Or else their parents might call an administrator to insist on why the student's individual learning need requires a special accommodation, maybe an A–.

That takes me to the second reason: Being raised by those helicopter parents on steroids. Even after they arrive in the workplace, Gen Zers are still only a phone call (or text) away from their parents. It is unlikely that their parents are still enforcing a bedtime (perhaps that one is unfortunate), but I would bet some of your less than tardy Gen Zers may still be receiving an actual wake-up call from a parent in the morning. Even worse, maybe they are on their own now, for the first time, after being reared by parents (and their parenting posses) who did all the work for them of closely scheduling, managing, and supporting their every move. With their parents doing so much of the work, many Gen Zers never mastered the basics of taking care of themselves.

Third, the customization of everything has entrenched in Gen Zers a fundamental expectation that individual accommodation is the norm. Even if they, themselves, did not home-school, never had an ILP (an "individual learning plan," very common in schools nowadays), and never took meds for their special "diagnosis," they surely grew up among kids who did. And surely too many people told them each and all, way too often, "You are a special case." Meanwhile, there has long been a growing current of personal customization in every sphere where consumers dwell—especially media. Of course, all of this dovetails with the long-term zeitgeist swing toward relativism, that is, "all styles are equally valid."

Gen Zers' basic assumption is that they should be able to just "be themselves" and "express" their true identity at work, even if that might include stuff like failing to follow through on a day when they are "just not feeling it."

Fourth, when it comes to Gen Zers' people skills, it is easy to blame the fact that they have become so accustomed to electronic communication that they are losing the ability to communicate well in-person. That's surely a big part of the story. Communication practices are habits, and most Gen Zers are in the habit of remote informal staccato and relatively low-stakes interpersonal communication because of their constant use of hand-held devices and social media and instant messaging. But there is much more going on here than Gen Zers staring at their devices too much, sending too many texts, and becoming increasingly less articulate because they have so little practice having real conversations. As a partner in a large accounting/consulting firm put it so well, "It's not just how they communicate that is the problem. It's what they have to say that really pisses me off!"

Fifth, much of what older, more experienced people might see as matters of professionalism—attitude, self-presentation, schedule, and interpersonal communication—Gen Zers are more likely to consider highly personal matters of individual style or preference and really none of their employer's business.

An experienced nurse-manager on a busy hospital floor told me about her campaign to stop the new young nurses from using their hand-held devices at the same time they are administering care to patients. The manager and her nursing supervisors had been surprised and impressed to discover how often the young nurses on their devices were instant messaging with each other about the patient care. They were asking each other for—and giving to each other—regular advice and support throughout the day. Sometimes, they were searching the Internet for clinical information, often reaching out on social media to other nurses who were not even co-workers. One supervisor was startled to discover a young nurse having a real-time video conference on her hand-held device with her friend, a nurse in India. "She was standing outside this patient's room, discussing the case with her friend in India. When I asked her about it later, she said this friend had been a mentor to her in school and she felt like she didn't have anyone here yet she could confide in." By the way, the nurse-manager hastened to add that the young nurse in question was NOT herself of Indian decent. She went on, "They spent a lot of time on Facetime together. She was more comfortable getting answers from her friend in India than turning to any of us for help."

2. OLD-FASHIONED "CRITICAL THINKING"

Why are today's young people not better at "thinking on their feet"—learning, problem solving, and decision making in their own heads without a device?

What managers tell us regularly in our interviews is summed up well by one senior-level nurse-manager with more than three decades of experience managing young nurses: "They just don't think on their feet the way they used to. They know a lot. But if they are not sure of something, they go right to their device. If there is not an obvious online resource to answer their question immediately, then they turn right to another person—whoever is available—another nurse, a doctor, or anyone they run into next. What they never seem to do is just stop and think. They can often find the 'right' answer, but often they don't fully understand the answer they've found. It's not just a lack of experience. It's a different way of thinking—shallow and wide, instead of digging deep. They don't puzzle through the problem, and they don't stop and reflect on why the right solution is the right solution."

As they become adult players in the real world of work, why don't they stop and think on their feet, puzzle through problems, and reflect more on the best solutions?

Of course, there is one big reason: They have never had the need. Today's information environment offers infinite answers to every question under the sun, and they've always had powerful, easy-to-use information technology at their fingertips all the time.

On this subject, I often remind older, more experienced people: "Do you remember when we used to have conversations with very smart people about meaningful things that sometimes ended with a giant chorus of 'I don't know,' 'I don't know,' 'I don't know,' and 'Neither do I'? Or maybe you remember having those 'I wonder if ____' conversations with yourself." Are you old enough to remember those conversations? Well, Gen Zers are not! They have never had that conversation—with themselves or with anyone else. As long as they can remember, when they reach that point in a conversation—"I wonder if ____"—they (or someone else) would go immediately to a hand-held device to find answers or a short related video or a giant detour that distracts them from the original inquiry altogether. Or they would ask the ultimate authority on everything—their parents.

With computers, content providers, and grown-ups to do so much of their thinking for them, Gen Zers have hardly any experience digging deep, puzzling, and reflecting. They have a built-in expectation that learning curves are instant. They think of learning in small increments, filling skill and knowledge gaps as they run across them. The long learning curve is a rarity and a bit of a mystery to Gen Z.

When it comes to the learning habits of Gen Zers, many experts blame changes in the emphasis of the education system at all levels: Teaching to the test has become too common. It is all too rare that schools are teaching students to assemble and evaluate evidence, construct multiple competing arguments and understand multiple sides in a debate, untangle seeming inconsistencies, and wrestle with complexity. In college, university, and graduate school, those learning technical skills are likely to continue throughout their education on that "learning for the test" pedagogical trajectory. Those being schooled in the liberal arts often err all the way on the other end of the spectrum. Young liberal arts graduates may become so convinced that "all styles are equally valid" they have difficulty vetting information for legitimacy, use value, and broader implications in the real world.

This takes me to another disturbing factor in today's information environment: the proliferation of half-baked experts spewing content on just about everything. Nowadays, you can find an expert to support nearly any proposition: "My expert says that two plus two equals five." What is one supposed to do with information like that? Yet information like that is everywhere. The impact of this factor goes way beyond the common Internet search misfire in which Gen Zers find the answer, but the answer is "two plus two equals five." Far more damaging, the organic pluralism of the Internet has led to a false sense of intellectual pluralism, a world in which people think, "Maybe two plus two does equal five." This has led to profound distortions in the public discourse—in all media—in which pure fiction, gut feelings, and opinions are given the same weight as well-researched facts, rigorous analysis, and strongly constructed arguments. This phenomenon dovetails with the swing of the zeitgeist pendulum toward cultural relativism more generally and the weakening of institutional credibility. After all, what authority figure in what institution has the staying power to say, definitively, that "two plus two must equal four"?

Maybe we shouldn't be so shocked when Gen Zers sometimes tell us, "It appears that two plus two may actually equal five." After all, in virtual reality, this equation probably has very few negative consequences. It's only now that they are entering the real world of the workplace where, suddenly, their lack of skill and experience in the basics of critical thinking can have very real consequences.

3. Old-Fashioned "Followership"

Why don't young people today "respect authority"? By the time they were growing up, "Question Authority!" was not a slogan anymore but a hackneyed cliché. So maybe it is too easy to explain away Gen Zers' seeming disregard for joining something larger and making personal sacrifices for the greater good.

Why don't Gen Zers value citizenship, service, and teamwork? Four reasons:

First, they think like customers. Yes, they know that their employers are the ones paying them. But still, they look at their relationship with any established institution, no matter how small or how large, and they think: "What do you have for me? And what currency do I need to use to get what I want/need from you?"

It's not that most Gen Zers are not feeling very fortunate just to be employed. They are. However, that gratitude is not bottomless nor is it without conditions. They are grateful to have a source of income and perhaps some benefits. They are grateful to be accepted, validated, wanted. They are grateful to have access to a hub of resources from which to acquire experience, training, networking; a place to be, with computers and phones and bathrooms; maybe a kitchen or a gym; maybe some office supplies. They are grateful for the future doors that might be opened by this current job. But let's not get carried away. It's not like they are likely to be here for a long time anyway.

Gen Zers may seem clueless about a lot of things, but they know very well that they are much less likely than those of prior generations to make long-term uninterrupted careers with one organization. They are also less likely to be exclusively employed by one organization at any given time. And they are less likely to work full-time and on-site. They are less likely to trust the "system" or the organization to take care of them and, thus, less likely to show what looks like loyalty—a desire to belong, deference to authority, a willingness to make short-term sacrifices for the good of the whole, and an eagerness to contribute regardless of credit or rewards.

Second is the way they think about their relationships with co-workers not in positions of authority: Gen Zers are simply not accustomed to sustained interactions with a group of "peers" who are

- Not all roughly their own age, and
- Not relationships of their own choosing, and
- Not refereed constantly, and
- Not also engaging with them in a parallel conversation through social media.

These relationships are real-world, involve a high degree of inter-dependency in pursuit of concrete goals every step of the way, and the stakes are high. Adults are in the workplace to earn their livelihoods. So there are lots of opportunities to disappoint and/or be disappointed.

Third is how they look at individuals in positions of authority—especially authority figures in institutions in which they are constituents. Once again, they think like customers. In this case, specifically, your customer!

Remember, Gen Zers love grown-ups! They have been and remain closer to their parents—and their parenting "posses"—than any other generation has ever been! The problem is that their parents, teachers, and counselors have always treated them like "little emperors." It's even worse if they are coming to you straight from a college or university, where Gen Zers were, in fact, actually the customers of the staff and faculty who were their proximate authority figures. Gen Zers look at older, more experienced people and presume on a very deep level that you are there to take care of them. Surely you wouldn't be interacting with them if you did not want to help them meet their basic needs and wants. They expect you to greet them warmly, make them feel comfortable, set them up for success, provide them with the resources they need, help them avoid pitfalls, and give them lots of encouragement. Isn't that what grown-ups do?

Gen Zers don't typically look at other people in the workplace trying to figure out "their proper place" in the context—how to adapt in order to "fit in" with others who clearly have longstanding relationships and a well-established course of dealing. Instead, they look at you—and everyone else in the room—and think: "I wonder what role you might play in this chapter of my life story?"

Fourth, Gen Zers are not planning to follow the old-fashioned career path, so they figure they are probably just passing through your organization anyway. Why go to a whole lot of trouble adapting to your approach to how they should manage themselves when they won't even be here that long? They are thinking: "Seriously, what am I supposed to do? Adapt my schedule and work habits and style and attitude for every new job?" Even if they could be convinced to adapt for an employer eventually, they are very unlikely to be ready to do it from the get-go, certainly not early in their first or second real jobs.

One large retail chain I know has a longstanding tradition of involving retail sales personnel in all aspects of the business, ranging from creative work, such as providing input on marketing, to janitorial work, such as cleaning the bathrooms in the store; and everything in between, including buying, inventory management, accounting, legal, HR, safety, loss prevention, and you name it. An executive in the company explained to me: "Of course, we have all those roles in the company: We have a professional marketing team, buyers, inventory managers, accountants, lawyers, and so on. We do use a janitorial service; they are not on their own cleaning the store. But we have a deep commitment to involving the store personnel in everything we do. We talk a lot about cross-training and teamwork. We do it because they are the face of the company to our customers and we want them to own everything in the organization." The executive added: "That's also one of the ways we recruit internally for corporate positions—not only store managers or district or regional, but also for other jobs throughout the organization." What's the problem? According to this executive, "The new young people only want to do what they want to do. They want to sit on the marketing panels, but they don't want to clean the store or change over inventory because those things happen after hours and seem less glamorous. They beg for the high-profile, fun, or interesting projects, but they complain bitterly when they are asked to help clean the store or change over inventory. Quite a few of them outright refuse to do it. Quite a few have been fired or have quit over it." As a result, the executive concluded, "We are currently rethinking our whole approach to these cross-training/teamwork projects."

Face the Hard Realities of the Soft Skills Gap

Maybe you are thinking: "Wait a minute. I know some young people who are great at professionalism, critical thinking, and followership!" Of course you do! And I do, too! It seems like now is a good time for me to make it clear that, even nowadays, there are many young people with excellent soft skills. It's just that there are not enough of them—it's a supply and demand thing. That's especially true among young people with in-demand technical skills, among whom there is a shortage to begin with. Over and over again, we hear from leaders and managers at all levels that the soft skills gap is not going away. If anything, it is getting worse. And it's not just about the youngest people in the workplace. Overall, this gap has been developing for decades. The costs are great, the opportunity costs are even greater, and yet the problem stands right there in plain sight, not even hiding. Why does this problem evade solutions?

There are three reasons:

First, you cannot hire your way around the soft skills gap, at least not entirely. If you are hiring for a low-supply high-demand technical-skill job, you probably won't be able to select out all those with weak soft skills. If you are hiring for non-technical jobs, then soft skills are among the only criteria, making the demand for those with strong soft skills very high, despite the low supply.

Second, soft skills cannot be spoon fed to young people or forced upon them. Soft skills are all about the regulation of the self. They must be fully embraced in order to be learned. You have to help Gen Zers to care enough about soft skills that their self-building drive is turned on and focused on mastering the missing soft skills.

Third, you probably don't have a lot of extra time or resources to pull your Gen Zers out of work and send them for soft skills training, or to create your own Boot Camp (like the Marines) to break down new workers and systematically rebuild them. If you are like most managers, then you deal with soft skill gap issues when they arise: when an employee is late, or inappropriate, or makes an error in judgment, or there are conflicts on the team, or there is a bad customer service interaction. You deal with the problem. Maybe you note the issue. Maybe if it is a recurring ongoing issue with an employee, you really drill down and try to deal with the problem. In any case, unless you are the rare exception, your approach to dealing with the soft skills gap is probably ad hoc, hit or miss.

Senior leaders in U.S. intelligence agencies have been grappling with the impact of steadily rising zero- to five-year employee turnover rates among new young intelligence professionals. This is a particularly pressing issue because intelligence agencies make an unusually large investment in new hires due to the elaborate selection criteria, the need to gain security clearance, the extensive requisite training, and the sensitive nature of the work and information to which employees are often privy. So it is a big problem when that investment walks out the door before the new young professionals have a chance to contribute to the mission. One intelligence official told me: "No matter how hard we try to develop a profile to help us select for retention—to predict who will be longer-term employees—it just doesn't work. We used to be able to do it. But it doesn't work anymore. Maybe there is no 'type' anymore who stays or a 'type' who goes. I'm afraid that the young people joining now who serve long-term will end up that way, not by deciding that today, but instead by deciding every few months or years to not leave just yet. We are making a lot of adjustments. But how are we supposed to identify the right high potentials to start developing for new leadership roles? It makes succession planning very difficult. Too often, those identified for promotion end up deciding to leave, taking with them the huge investment we've made in them."

In our training seminars, when I start talking about these difficult realities, managers start nodding their heads and listening carefully. I often say, "I don't have any easy answers because easy answers work only in fantasyland. What I do have is a lot of difficult partial solutions." That's when managers in the real world know that I really have something to offer them. All I do in my seminars is teach managers how to imitate the best practices that the most effective managers are doing successfully every single day. How are the most effective managers bridging the soft skills gap every day?

Here's the number one thing they have in common: They recognize the incredible power of soft skills—in themselves and in others and in organizations and teams. They understand what can go wrong when individuals or teams or organizations have big gaps in their soft skills. Even more important, they understand how much can go so incredibly right—the extraordinary potential for added value—as a result of unlocking the power of soft skills.

Chapter 2

You Can't Hire Your Way Around the Soft Skills Gap

You can shine a bright light on soft skills in every aspect of your human capital management practices:

◆ Staffing strategy and hiring
◆ On-boarding and up-to-speed training
◆ Performance management and talent development
◆ Ongoing training
◆ Management and leadership

But you simply cannot hire your way around the soft skills gap.

There are many sectors of the labor market in which significant education and credentials are not required threshold criteria for employment—these include many service or quasi-service jobs in retail, restaurant, cleaning, warehousing, moving, mining, agriculture, and so forth. The young talent pool available to these sectors offers many "diamonds in the rough," but few fully refined, when it comes to soft skills. Yes, you can (and should) poach the most polite cashier, waiter, janitor, or other person from your competition across the street, but that strategy only goes so far. Even your best hires in this sector will require significant on-boarding and up-to-speed training—not just in the basic tasks of the job—but also in your high priority soft skills.

At the next tier of the skill spectrum is the sector of the labor market in which substantial technical training may be required, but may be done in less than a year. Sometimes this training is provided by a public or private vocational education program, often affiliated with local employers. In other cases, employers provide pre-employment training or extensive on-the-job training. These jobs range from construction and assembly and mechanical repair work to book-keeping to food preparation to sales. These programs are intended to provide "job-ready" employees. What always amazes me about the training for these roles is how they focus almost exclusively on the hard skills and pay only lip service to soft skills training. Then they complain bitterly about the soft skills of these new employees, especially the youngest among them.

At the highest end of the labor market, the very threshold criteria for employment include years of education and formal training. If you are hiring engineers, doctors, nurses, medical technicians, accountants, actuaries, financial advisers, law enforcement officers, teachers, data analysts, code makers, code breakers, enterprise level management, and so many other roles for which the supply is far below demand, then you are squarely in the middle of the technical skill gap that captures so much of the attention in the media. It takes so much time, energy and money—so much personal investment on the part of the individual employee—to acquire these in-demand skills that employers are in fierce competition for them. Employers often have so few candidates with the requisite hard skills that they simply cannot rule people out because of seeming gaps in their soft skills. Of course, no matter how highly trained they may be in the hard skills, new employees still require on-boarding and up-to-speed training in the systems, policies, and practices of their new employer. Again, I am always amazed at how little attention is given to soft skills training in the on-boarding and up-to-speed training process.

The bad news punch-line in this quick lesson on contemporary labor market dynamics is that you cannot hire your way around the soft skills gap and, therefore, you simply must plan to address it in every aspect of your human capital management. The good news corollary is that you can hire smarter and give yourself a competitive advantage by making some slight adjustments in your staffing strategy, recruiting, and selection of new employees.

Staffing Strategy and Hiring

Yes, you need to hire people who have or can learn the required technical skills. Yes, if you are hiring at the high end, you have no choice but to hire those who have acquired the necessary education and training. Yes, there is a limited supply. No, that doesn't mean you can ignore soft skills in your hiring.

Nowadays, all the attention in the talent wars is going to the technical skill gap. Yet, every day in our work, the stories managers tell us about good hires gone bad, and bad hires gone worse, are about failures in the soft skills, not the hard skills. That's true in every sector. It is rare that managers tell us a new hire failed because of a lack of technical skills. Nine times out ten, an unsuccessful hire fails due to soft skills, not hard.

Never forget, one very good hire is much better than three or four or five mediocre hires. No matter where you are on the skill spectrum, build in soft skills criteria systematically in every aspect of your staffing strategy and hiring process:

Step One

For every single position, build a profile and job description that includes not just the key hard skills for that role, but also the key soft skills. Use our competency model to start your brainstorming, but make them your own. Once you identify the high priority soft skill behaviors for each position, name them yourself. Describe them in detail. Build those criteria into the basic job requirements in no uncertain terms from the very outset. Be prepared to turn away candidates who do not meet these soft skill criteria, just as you would turn away candidates without the necessary hard skills. Or, if you are forced to hire people without the required soft skills, make sure you have a plan in place to address those soft skill gaps from the first day of employment, just as you would have a plan in place if you hired an employee without the necessary technical skills.

Step Two

Look for talent from sources well known for the strong soft skills you need. If you are hiring out of schools and training programs, definitely find out which ones include soft skills in their standard curriculum. If you are poaching talent from other employers, poach from employers known for their strong soft skills training. This is why so many employers want to hire those who have served in the military: You can be sure that most people who have served successfully in the military will display respect for authority, willingness to wear a uniform, excellent manners, timeliness, consistency, follow-through, teamwork, and initiative. The same goes for anybody who makes it to Eagle Scout. Maybe it is the Peace Corps, or an NGO, a club or a church or an athletic team; maybe you are looking for someone who has run a marathon or been a camp counselor or a school teacher or volunteered in a soup kitchen. What schools, employers, or organizations do you know where members or alumni are likely to have stronger soft skills in the areas that matter the most to you? Create a shorthand list of "clearinghouse" talent sources, successful participation in which is an indicator that job candidates are likely to have stronger soft skills. Then pay special attention to candidates with those soft skills "credentials" on top of their hard skills credentials. But don't wait for them to come to you. Be proactive about seeking candidates from those sources. Look for candidates If you can build relationships with key influencers in those sources—teachers, career counselors, leaders, active members of organizations, military outplacement personnel, and so forth. They can help you identify good candidates, which also gives them a positive reputation for helping good people find good jobs.

STEP THREE

Include your high priority soft skills behaviors in your employer branding and recruitment campaign messaging. That's why it's so important to name your high priority soft skills—to have meaningful slogans to capture them. Of course, there is always the iconic "the few, the proud, the Marines" as an example. That message is a signal to applicants that this job is going to be very demanding of them on a very deep level. Your recruitment message says a lot about how you see yourself as an employer. If you advertise for automobile mechanics by saying, "hiring qualified automobile mechanics," you are not really saying much. If your message is "looking for very smart automobile mechanics who are great team players," that says a lot more. Remember, the goal of any recruiting campaign is to deliver a compelling message in order to draw a sufficiently large applicant pool so that you can be very selective. Your goal is not necessarily to draw applicants who are all "very smart" and "great team players" but, at the very least, you want to draw applicants who aspire to be very smart and aspire to be great team players. You want to draw applicants who are looking for a job in which they can learn and grow and build themselves up. We call it a "self-building" job. You want to draw applicants for whom the idea of "self-building" is a big turn-on, not a turn-off.

STEP FOUR

Start with a bias against hiring: Look for red flags. The biggest mistake hiring managers make—especially when hiring for low-supply high-demand technical skills—is continuing the "attraction campaign" until the job candidate has accepted the job, and sometimes until the new employee is already at work. We call this "selling candidates all the way in the door." In a tight labor market, the pressure to hire leads to hard-selling a job to a candidate, even if that person is not ideal for the job. In fact, so many employers are so starved for young talent that they just can't bear to turn potential employees away, even in the face of huge red flags. If someone comes late for the interview or falls asleep during the interview or has typos in his résumé—and timeliness, good health, or attention to detail are important soft skills for this job—then those red flags are telling you, "DON'T HIRE THIS PERSON!"

STEP FIVE

Build a selection process that places a heavy emphasis on high priority soft skills. Here's a short-cut: Scare away young job candidates who only think they are serious by shining a bright light on all the downsides of the job. If you need to hire nurses with especially high levels of grit and patience, make sure to tell them early in the selection process that they will sometimes be expected to help orderlies change bedpans. If you need to hire engineers with especially high levels of diligence, make sure to tell them right away there will be plenty of late nights and weekends coming very soon. Whatever the worst, most difficult aspects of the job may be, start your selection process with vivid descriptions of those downsides. Then see which candidates are still interested in the job. They are the ones worth testing and interviewing.

We recommend using research-validated testing whenever possible to get a quick baseline reading of an applicant's aptitude in key areas of the job, including high priority soft skills. Whatever test you settle on, just make sure you can implement and evaluate it with relative speed. And make sure you know in advance exactly what you are looking for. What are you testing for? If you need an employee who can write well, simply hand the applicant a piece of paper and ask him to write something. If you need an employee who can speak well, ask her to prepare a brief presentation and then present it. If you need an employee who can solve problems in spatial relations, give her a puzzle. If you need an employee who can solve math problems, give him some math problems to solve. If you need an employee who can be on time, schedule three interviews, at three different times. And so on. Of course, some soft skills are harder to test for than others.

Then comes the job interview, the one employment selection process almost every manager does, but very few do well. When it comes to interviewing, the best practice is still the simple model of behavioral interviewing. Although there are entire courses taught in behavioral interviewing, I often teach it to managers in my seminars in three minutes. Behavioral interviewing simply means asking applicants to tell you a story and then listening carefully to the story. When you are doing behavioral interviewing, make sure to ask applicants, not only about their use of hard skills, but also their use of soft skills: "Tell me a story about a time you solved a problem at work" or "Tell me a story about a conflict you had with another employee at work. How did you solve it?"

Finally, consider one last stage of selection, we call "the realistic job preview." This might be a probationary hiring period, or a pre-real job internship, during which you can try out the employee and the employee can try out the job for a while. Make sure to assign the person real tasks that mirror the actual tasks, responsibilities, and projects he or she will be asked to do if he or she accepts the job. Make sure to include the grunt work. Another option is a period of "job shadowing" or "tagging along" with another person in your organization who is doing the same job this person will be doing if hired. This approach is sometimes used in hospitals. Make sure that the would-be health care workers get to see sick patients, bedpans being emptied, and some of the other tough tasks they'll have to handle. By tagging along for several days, a week or more, your applicant will obtain a good picture of what the job entails.

You will also get the double bonus of having the existing employee who is shadowed spend a lot of time with the applicant in the job setting. This often leads to existing employees coming in and saying, "Hey, I hope we are going to hire this person!" or "Hey, we are not going to hire this person, are we?" Such feedback will tell you a lot. If applicants can't job-shadow, perhaps you can give them an opportunity to watch people doing the actual job—either in person or on video. Sometimes on factory floors or in restaurant kitchens, the best thing you can do is let a prospective employee watch people actually doing the work for a little while and make sure he knows what he is getting into.

STEP SIX

If there is any lag time between the time an offer is made and accepted and day one of the actual job, take advantage of that time. Perhaps the employee needs to finish school or the employer must complete a security screening. Use the delay to keep sending the message about your high priority soft skill behaviors: Send books or videos or other targeted learning materials. In every way you can, keep sending the message that those soft skill behaviors really matter.

On-Boarding and Up-to-Speed Training

Ask yourself: What happens when your new young employees walk through the door on day one? How do you leverage those first days and weeks?

You won't be surprised that my platinum standard for onboarding and up-to-speed training is the Marine's Boot Camp. For thirteen solid weeks, they provide an all-encompassing 24/7 experience in which they take an ordinary human being and transform that person into a Marine—a person with a unique set of self-management skills, problem-solving skills, and people skills—a person so connected to the Marine Corps and its mission and every other Marine that this person is now ready to walk into the line of fire, literally, and win battles.

You don't need obstacle courses and firing ranges. You don't need to make your newly hired employees do push-ups in the sand in the middle of the night. But take the lesson: What message are you sending about standards and expectations for high priority behaviors from day one?

First, make sure you know exactly what happens with your new hires in the formal orientation, on-boarding, and up-to-speed training. Most employers have only a minimal process for welcoming new employees and getting them on-board and up-to-speed. Obviously, some employers are better at this than others. Typically, employers provide a basic introduction to the mission and history of the organization (or not), they give the basic facts and figures (or not), have new employees meet some of the key players (or not), receive a primer in the policies and paperwork (or not), and maybe some of the rules and traditions (or not).

Second, consider the inevitable hand-off to the hiring manager (maybe that is you), once the official orientation program is complete. That's where so much of the real on-boarding action is going to happen, and that's exactly where the ball is so often dropped. Don't drop that ball.

If you want to send the message that those behaviors are truly a high priority, then you have to pay more than lip service. How much of your on-boarding and up-to-speed training is dedicated to spelling out performance standards and expectations for those high priority soft skill behaviors? How much time is dedicated to championing those behaviors and teaching them?

Here's a pretty simple rule: It should be about half.

As one savvy leader in a very successful retail chain put it to me: "For every hour we spend teaching a cashier how to operate the register, we spend at least an hour teaching her customer service skills—how to interact with customers and how to solve their problems."

Of course, it doesn't have to be half and half. Maybe the best approach is to have a dynamic integrated approach to on-boarding and up-to-speed training that is designed in every way to send a powerful message about high standards and expectations for employees' attitudes and behavior in relation to work.

One of my favorite companies is a rental car company that prides itself on hiring only college graduates for every position, no matter how entry level. They also pride themselves on an on-boarding process that not only teaches every new hire the business, but also makes it 1,000 percent clear to new hires exactly what kind of workplace citizenship is expected of every single employee. On top of hours upon hours of training, with computer based tools and hands-on coaches, new hires can expect to find themselves out in the parking lot washing cars. Everybody—from the top to the bottom—in this organization is expected to wash cars. Nobody is too important to wash cars. In between washing cars, new hires are expected to study. And study they do, because each week they must demonstrate proficiency in a range of subjects, including the company's computer system, details about the company's fleet, insurance, reservations, sales, marketing, customer service, billing, administration, decision making with everyday situations, corporate philosophy, and on and on.

The training materials spell out everything new hires must learn from week to week. And they study every night because—from day one—they are expected to be working, helping out in any way they can, during the day. There are also weekly coaching sessions with a fellow employee; each new hire is assigned a coach. There are tests at the thirty-day mark, at sixty days, and at ninety days. This incredibly impressive program, which the company runs on the job in thousands of rental car shops all over the world, teaches new hires not just how to run the business, but also inculcates a powerful sense of the kind of work ethic and commitment the company requires. The results can be seen in every corner of this world-class organization. Their on-boarding program is not exactly the Marine Corps Boot Camp, but it is truly profound in its impact.

Of course, on-boarding and up-to-speed training needn't be profound. Let me give you a more mundane example. In one large company that hires a lot of new young engineers, managers and more experienced engineers were increasingly frustrated with some of the work habits of many of their new young engineers, including their email communication habits. A senior director of engineering in this company told me: "When it came to email, they did a bunch of things that drove everybody crazy: They would do every email 'no no': red flag emails indiscriminately, cc too many people on emails, or reply all to the wrong things, fail to change subject lines. But in particular they would send lots of very short email messages from their hand-held devices instead of composing a proper email. We developed a list of do's and don'ts for email communication and we built in a thirty-minute module in orientation." How did that work? "Problem solved."

I have a very similar story from a top accounting firm. Managers in this firm had noticed a growing pattern of "poor meeting manners" among new young staff accountants. What are "poor meeting manners"? According to one senior partner: "Poor attendance, late arrival, constantly looking at their devices, lack of preparation, interrupting, going way off topic, making inappropriate comments . . . I could go on." The solution was very similar: The firm began explicitly teaching new hires how to prepare for and conduct themselves in meetings. It was so successful that the firm leadership decided to overhaul everybody's "meeting manners." As it turned out, it wasn't just the new associates whose meeting manners were not so great. After they developed the "meeting manners" program, the leadership realized that everybody in the firm could benefit from learning and observing these best practices for meetings. As a result, said the senior partner, "We had a real change in our culture around meetings. People in this firm became religious about following the rules of conduct. Our meetings got much better, and they remain so. It's a centerpiece of our culture now."

Gee, maybe that's mundane and profound at the same time.

Performance Management and Talent Development

Most large organizations have some sort of formalized performance management system, and nowadays more and more are extending those systems to also take a more structured approach to talent development. The essence of performance management and talent development is simple. It's all about continuous improvement:

- ◆ Setting clear goals
- ◆ Monitoring and measuring actual performance in relation to those goals
- ◆ Providing feedback, direction, and guidance
- ◆ Problem solving and troubleshooting
- ◆ Identifying opportunities to speed up or increase quality
- ◆ Recognizing and rewarding success
- ◆ Identifying high performers for key assignments, opportunities, and promotions

Organizations with formalized systems typically start with annual or quarterly corporate goals and then cascade those larger goals down the chain of command to each division, department, team, and individual. This is to create alignment from the top to the bottom so that everybody is moving in the same direction at the same time. In any case, at the individual level, employees typically spell out goals for themselves—annual goals and quarterly goals, and if they are smart, then they take the process further to monthly and weekly and maybe even daily goals. Usually, these goals are primarily focused on key performance indicators—revenue or profitability, maybe, or else productivity (output) or quality (negative error rate)—related to the individual employee's specific tasks, responsibilities, and projects. While soft skill behaviors have a huge impact on any individual's performance when it comes to key performance indicators, the specific behaviors may not be spelled out explicitly or identified as specific goals in a performance management system.

Usually, when soft skill behaviors are spelled out—if at all—in a formal performance management system would be in one of two cases:

1. If an employee is failing to meet performance goals, then corrective measures might be spelled out in terms of an employee's specifically related sub-optimal soft skills behaviors. The problem is that, often, by this point it's already too late. If you wait until an employee has demonstrated a track record of failure on a key soft skill behavior, then the performance management system is probably going to serve simply as a way to document that failure and provide a paper trail to help fire that person.
2. Soft skill behaviors might be included as part of an individual's personal goals and/or for "professional development." The problem is that this often is the part of the employee's performance goals that are given the least weight and the least attention. Employees are likely to give these goals weight and attention in direct proportion to how much the organization does.

As a seasoned leader in a top financial services firm told me: "Your people can tell whether you really take this stuff seriously and they can tell if you don't. If you measure it, they pay attention. If there are consequences for failure, they pay attention. If there are rewards for success, they pay attention. When you identify top performers, the smart ones look and see, 'What makes that person successful?' If that person is rewarded and promoted despite their failures on those soft skills, people pay attention to that. They say, 'Oh, if you make your numbers, that's what really matters.' But if you hold people back when they fail on those soft skills, despite making the numbers, then people pay attention to that, too. What you measure and what has consequences and what gets rewarded, that's what your people are going to focus on."

Your employees can only focus on so many things at once. And you can only focus on so many things at once. If high priority behaviors are truly high priorities, then you must make that clear with real stakes in your performance management and talent development. Whether you have a formalized system or not, remember, whatever you measure and what has consequences and what gets rewarded, that is what they are going to focus on.

If you want your employees to really focus on high priority soft skill behaviors, then you need to:

◆ Set clear goals for specific behaviors
◆ Monitor and measure each employee's actual performance on those specific behaviors in relation to those goals
◆ Provide candid feedback, direction, and guidance on those behaviors
◆ Problem solve and troubleshoot when course correction is necessary
◆ Identify opportunities to improve on those specific behaviors
◆ Recognize and reward success on those specific behaviors
◆ Identify high performers for key assignments, opportunities, and promotions based on success on those specific behaviors

Your employees need to know exactly what is expected and required of them when it comes to high priority soft skills behaviors— every step of the way. They also need to know that their performance will be measured and that the score will have real consequences for failure and real rewards for success.

Ongoing Training

Now I should say, "I have good news and bad news": If you succeed in getting your employees focused on building up their performance on high priority soft skills, then the next questions they are going to ask is: "Exactly what training resources can you provide me for improving in these areas?" That is both the good news and the bad news.

Why is it bad news?

One health care executive captured the explanation in simple terms: "We invest so much in education and training for our new young professionals that we have gotten a reputation among our competitors as a great place from which to poach talent. We invest in them through internal programs and also tuition reimbursement for everything from a one-day seminar to pursuing an advanced degree. It is a great tool for recruiting and morale. But it also paints a target on our back. The other hospitals in the region actively recruit our two-year employees. Of course, they are thinking, 'You've been working there for two years? Perfect. Come work for us and we'll get the return on their education and training investment. It's very frustrating!"

We call this the "development investment paradox." You invest in developing your new young talent only to make them more valuable in the free market, where they are in danger of selling your development investment to the highest bidder. This is problematic when it comes to hard skills training as well as soft skills training: But it is especially maddening with soft skills training because soft skills are broad, transferable skills that never become obsolete and will make your employees more valuable anywhere they go in any job. Plus, if you think of soft skills training as "extra" rather than "mission critical," then it seems like a foolish investment to make altogether.

What are the answers to this paradox?

1. First, use this paradox as an important reminder of the wisdom of sourcing new talent by targeting employers with great reputations for building up the soft skills of their new young employees.
2. Second, be prepared: If you become one of those employers known for building up the soft skills of your new young employees, you are going to become a target for talent poaching. Think of your competitors sitting around a table: "Their

front-line employees are so great. They seem so solid, well put together, smart, capable, polite, engaged, and engaging! What can we do to lure them away?" That's a problem you DO want to have. However, it puts a high premium on retaining the great young talent you are going to be developing.

3. Third, calibrate your development investment every step of the way so you never go too far out on a limb. But don't fool yourself: High priority soft skills behaviors ARE absolutely mission-critical. That's why it's so important to know precisely which behaviors are your high priorities and focus on them like a laser beam.

4. Fourth, you need to get your employees to really buy into the value of the high-priority behaviors so they really own the learning process and are prepared to share the costs of the investment. That means you need to engage their formidable self-building drive. If their self-building is engaged, they will spend lots of time on self-directed learning outside of work and, when they are at work, they will be purposely focused on demonstrating and practicing their growing repertoires on the job.

5. Fifth, provide them with as many easy-to-use targeted learning resources as you possibly can to support their self-directed learning. These can be low-tech resources just as much as high tech, but remember, they are going to be very tuned in to just-in-time learning resources available online. In particular, today's young talent is used to being able to get a simple tutorial on just about any topic by going straight to a short online video with explanatory articles (or multiple videos from multiple sources). If you want to have some input on the sources from which they learn, that means building and supporting easy-to-access learning resources that are in alignment with your training goals.

Does this all mean that you shouldn't be so generous when it comes to less targeted investments in soft skills? You have to do the math for yourself, but I will say this: Whatever investments you make, the key to protecting your investment is making your young employees full partners—co-investors—in the learning process. As long as they are actively learning skills they value (with your support) they are much less likely to think about leaving.

The general manager of a restaurant from a well-known chain recently shared this with me: "When we teach our team members customer service skills, obviously it's all about taking care of our customers. But a huge part of our emphasis is on the value to our employees as well. Sometimes, they don't realize at first that customer service skills are extremely valuable in any role in any organization. So we hammer away at the fact that every minute they spend learning and practicing customer service skills is not just an investment in this job but also an investment they are making in themselves. We need them to buy in, so we really sell it to them." How does it work? "It really works because we really help the team members own it: Every day there is a quick team huddle, and in every meeting a different team member takes a turn leading a quick customer service lesson. They can take a lesson from our curriculum or they are free to create their own lessons. They find cool videos and articles and quotes, and some of them really get into it. We take this very seriously, so we recognize and reward team members when they go above and beyond, financially and otherwise. We often add the lessons they create to our curriculum, and we give them full credit as content creators. It creates a virtuous cycle: Some of them really get into it, and they make a point of actively practicing the techniques on the job and really showing off what they are learning. Of course, they are usually the ones who stay and become assistant managers and start moving up through the company."

Lessons learned:

- *If you want them to buy in, then you have to really sell it to them:* Take the time to make the case for why the skills you want them to learn are not just good for you and your business, but are also going to be really valuable to them. Remember, soft skills are broad, highly transferable skills that are valuable in any kind of job and never become obsolete.
- *Help them own the learning by giving them a concrete role in the process:* How can you get them actively involved in the training? Can they bring some of their own ideas to the table? Can they help you define learning goals? Identify sources of content or create original content? Teach some of the lessons?

◆ *Make sure they have opportunities to practice what they are learning on the job and gain recognition and reward and advancement through active participation:* Pay close attention to the employees who really embrace it, as they are likely the ones who might stay and build careers in your organization.

Remember that Gen Zers are highly accustomed to self-directed learning. If they are eager to learn something, you cannot hold them back in today's information environment. They will go out into the endless sea of information and people online and navigate their own course of links and sources. Before you know it, they will be surprising you with their thoughtfulness, originality, and engagement in the learning.

Whether you are hiring people to wait tables in a restaurant, dig ditches, or engage in high-level sales, if you can help them to own the learning process, they are going to be thinking more and more about how they do whatever it is they do. Remember, knowledge work is not about what you do but about how you do whatever it is you do. If you help them make whatever they are doing knowledge work by constantly trying to leverage soft skills in their work, they are going to become more and more invested in that work; more and more engaged; and better and better at their jobs.

"As soon as they join my team, I have new team members develop their own individualized learning plan for targeted technical and non-technical learning," said one very smart manager in a large pharmaceutical company. "They need to learn our product line with all the technical specifications. But it's every bit as important that they learn how to show up very professional in their look and demeanor. They need to know how to get a doctor's attention and hold the doctor's attention. I want my reps to seem intelligent and sophisticated, not just knowledgeable about our products."

The pharma manager continued, "The funny thing is that, with the technical stuff, I can drill that into their heads. But with the soft skills, that's more like getting in shape. I can't go running and do push-ups for you. You need to go to the gym if you are going to get in shape. So the individualized learning plans are really great when it comes to the soft skills. I have them map out their learning goals in detail. For every goal, I have them go out and do research and create a list of learning resources. Those resources can be books, videos, people in real life or in their online social networks, article links, websites, or really anything else. That process alone—of doing that research—has quite an impact. They learn so much just going out and researching the learning resources. Then I have them make a learning plan with concrete learning goals and specific lessons related to the goals. They keep a learning log of the lessons they've done, the work product involved, if any, the learning goals they've accomplished, and how the learning is making a real impact on their actual work. This also becomes a regular part of our team meetings—sharing learning resources and sharing lessons."

What is the best part about this approach? "The best thing about this is that they do so much of the work of their own training. Plus, they are mining the Internet for learning resources, and usually the bulk of the resources they find are basically free. On top of that, they end up doing such a good job harnessing those resources, organizing them, and sharing them, that they are actually building up a great training library at practically no cost to the company. Some of the stuff they come up with is so good and so well targeted to what we need because they are motivated to find the right material to help them on the job. And they do most of it on their own time."

The Human Element: What Role Are You Going to Play?

This last section comes last, not because it is the least important, but rather because it is the most important. Whether you are in a large, complex organization with lots of resources or a tiny business where you are the chief cook and bottle washer, the most important element in bridging the soft skills gap is the human element.

If you are not an active champion of high priority soft skills behaviors in your sphere of influence and authority, then you can be sure that the young talent in your midst will not buy in. If key leaders are not walking the talk—and talking the walk—Gen Zers will simply roll their eyes at the best slogans and logos. No matter how vividly clear the messaging and training has been throughout the hiring and on-boarding process—even if key soft skill behaviors are part of their individual performance plans—if their leaders do not emulate the high priority behaviors themselves and emphasize them in their day-to-day management, Gen Zers will not believe the organization is serious. As much as they may seem to take their cues from peers or online sources, you can be sure that they will take their cues about what aspects of performance really matter from the authority figures with whom they interact most.

Sure, you need to get your young employees to own their soft skills learning process and make available lots of easy-to-use online resources so they can pursue their own self-directed learning. But that doesn't let you off the hook. You have to spend time with them—in person whenever possible—to lead them to the purposeful self-directed learning, and you have to spend time with them during the intervals between their self-directed learning sessions.

Remember: Gen Zers love grown-ups. They prefer to have a real person in the real world who is investing in their learning and growth—a real-life grown-up who is engaging with them, holding them accountable, and recognizing their success every step of the way. More important, the very nature of soft skills is such that they are very hard to develop without the help of another human being who can serve as an objective third-party observer and source of candid feedback. Ideally, that human being would be one who is a bit older and more experienced, perhaps one with greater influence and authority—one who can provide guidance, direction, and support.

What role are you—and other leaders in your organization—going to play in bridging the soft skills gap?

If you are leading, managing, or supervising any person on any project for any period of time, you have an obligation to provide regular guidance, direction, support, and coaching to that person on every aspect of that person's performance, including that person's performance on high priority soft skills behaviors. The problem is that it's so easy—in the day-to-day grind of work—to put these issues on the back burner. Most managers don't spend much time talking with their employees about their soft skills development, unless they are dealing with a specific instance of failure. Right? When do managers most often talk with their direct reports about matters of professionalism or critical thinking or followership? When an employee is late or dressed inappropriately or loses something or fails to follow through or makes a "stupid" mistake or curses at the wrong time or has a conflict with a customer or a co-worker . . . or something else that is a petty failure.

That's why managers often say things like, "Do I really have to talk to my employees about these things? They are adults. They should already know how to manage themselves and solve problems and play well with others." Sorry. You really have no choice. If you are in charge of anybody, then it is part of your job.

At the very least, you must build it into your regular management routine. Talk about the high priority soft skills in team meetings and talk about them in your ongoing one-on-one dialogue with every single person you manage. Focus on the high priority behaviors in your organization, your team, in each role, or those that are particular focal points for particular individuals. Trumpet the broad performance standards regularly. Just like every other aspect of performance: Require it. Measure it. Reward people when they do it. Hold people to account when they don't.

Become a Teaching Style Manager

Managers often ask me: "At what point can I back off on giving them so much attention?" My answer: "Whenever you want to start losing that employee's best efforts."

Surely some Gen Zers need more attention than others. But they all need your attention. The superstars want to be recognized and rewarded, but they also want managers who are in a position to help them do more, better, and faster and earn more for their hard work. Low performers are the only ones who don't want their managers' attention, but they need it more than anyone. And mediocre performers—the vast majority of employees who are somewhere in the middle of the performance spectrum— often don't know what they want from a manager. But the fastest way to turn a mediocre performer into a low performer is to leave that person alone without any guidance, direction, support, or coaching. Your job is to lift up all those employees and help them do more work—faster and better every step of the way. Not just because that's good for business, but also because continuous improvement is the key to keeping Gen Zers focused and motivated.

Gen Zers want managers who know who they are, know what they are doing, and are in a position to help. They want managers who spend enough time with them to teach them the tricks and the shortcuts, warn them of pitfalls, and help them solve problems. They want managers who are strong enough to support them through bad days and counsel them through difficult judgment calls. They want to know you are keeping track of their successes and helping them get better and better every day. That's what I call a "teaching style manager."

Being a "teaching style manager" means:

◆ Talk about what's going right, wrong, and average every step of the way.
◆ Remind everybody of broad performance standards regularly.
◆ Turn best practices into standard operating procedures, and teach them to everybody.
◆ Use plans and step-by-step checklists whenever possible.
◆ Focus on concrete actions within the control of the individual employee.
◆ Monitor, measure, and document individual performance in writing.
◆ Follow up, follow up, follow up, and provide regular candid feedback.
◆ Ask really good questions.
◆ Listen carefully.
◆ Answer questions.
◆ Get input.
◆ Learn from what your employees are learning on the front line.
◆ Think through potential obstacles and pitfalls and make back-up planning part of every work plan.
◆ Anticipate and prepare.
◆ Train and practice.
◆ Strategize together.
◆ Provide advice, support, motivation, and even inspiration once in a while.

Teaching-style management is also how you can help your most ambitious Gen Zers who are so eager to take on more and more challenges and responsibilities. Gen Zers often tell us, "I can do so much more than I am doing. I want to do so much more than I am doing. But I don't want to do more of the same. I want to do something new and different." While this desire is a valuable impulse on the part of self-starting Gen Zers, it also poses two significant challenges to their immediate managers:

1. First, their job is to get the work done, whatever the work happens to be. Sometimes there are no new and interesting challenges. But wait. That doesn't need to be the end of the discussion. Help them make their current work new and interesting by teaching them to leverage knowledge, skill, and wisdom to do their work better, whatever that work happens to be. As soon as they walk in the door, have all new employees create individualized learning plans in which they map out their responsibilities, and for each responsibility, make a list of learning resources (books, people, specific websites). Encourage them to set learning goals and then keep a journal of what they are learning and how they are using it on the job.

2. Second, if you have truly new and interesting challenges for Gen Zers, then you will have to make the time to teach them how to do that new and interesting work. You can't just give them a new challenge and say, "Figure it out." The secret is to teach and transfer just one small task/responsibility at a time. Make sure the person masters each new task/responsibility before you transfer another. You can train them the old-fashioned way in short-term stages that track directly with adjustments in their day-to-day responsibilities. Every new task turns into a proving ground, which enables them to demonstrate proficiency and earn more responsibility right away.

Don't fall for the myth that Gen Zers only want to learn from computers. That's nonsense. Remember, they love grown-ups. They want to learn from people. They want to learn from you. You will never really take the place of a parent, but if you can truly become a trusted teaching style manager, that is about as close as you can get.

Take It to the Next Level

If you want to take it the next level, go beyond regular performance coaching. Become a true champion of soft skills by becoming a teaching style leader. Make teaching/learning the soft skills basics an explicit part of your mission and goals for your team going forward.

I know this seems like way too much to take on for some managers. Maybe you are thinking: "I am not a teacher or trainer. And I certainly don't have the time—nor do my employees—to spend a bunch of time in soft skills training." Beware of this thinking. If you are reading this book, you are probably struggling with the soft skills gap in your organization or on your team.

The second half of this book is dedicated to helping you teach the missing basics—complete with step-by-step lesson plans. Imagine the impact you could have if you dedicated just one or two hours per week to building up the soft skills of your team. In just one or two hours per week, you can make them aware, make them care, and help them learn the missing basics one by one—one step at a time. You can build them up and make them so much better.

Chapter 3

Unlocking the Power of Soft Skills

So many business leaders and managers at all levels fall for the myth that soft skills are a "nice to have" rather than a "must have"—simply a luxury they cannot afford to prioritize. That is a huge mistake.

Hard skills are easier to define and measure, yes. Hard skills are critical and they deserve lots of attention, but don't let anybody fool you: Soft skills are every bit as important. For the vast majority of your workforce, soft skills are the key to your success in the workplace and competitive differentiation in the marketplace. Soft skills are the source of a huge amount of power that is always right there hiding in plain sight—a tremendous reservoir of often untapped value—a secret weapon for any smart organization, team, leader, or individual performer.

Yes, the hard skills—the technical skills—are absolutely required in any job. That's every bit as true at the low end of the skill spectrum as it is at the high end. Right? Even if you are a cashier in a convenience store, you simply must know how to operate the cash register and make change to do the job. That's the bare minimum. After all, you can't do the job if you can't do the job. But that's only half the story.

The many soft skills I put into those three old fashioned buckets—professionalism, critical thinking, and followership—are where even the most technically proficient employees in any field can go terribly wrong—or incredibly right.

Imagine the cashier who is always early, bright-eyed, cheerful, moves through transactions swiftly and steadily, all the while greeting customers warmly and crisply, up-selling enthusiastically, answering customer questions accurately and concisely, and solving customer problems whenever they arise, and, when there are no customers waiting, keeping everything clean and organized behind the counter, jumping in to help others, and always watching that counter in case a customer is approaching.

Think about it: Even if the cashier can operate the cash register and make correct change, there is a big difference between a cashier who is always a little bit early to work and doesn't take long breaks and one who is chronically late or disappears for long stretches of time. There is a big difference between the cashier who is bright-eyed and the one who is bleary-eyed; the one who is smiling and the one who is rolling his eyes; the one who can help a customer when something is wrong with his order and one who is clueless; the one who is staring at her device and talking with her peers behind the counter and the one who pays attention to the customer; the one who mumbles and the one who says enthusiastically, "Would you like a beverage today, sir?"

These differences may not be thrilling and sexy, but they matter. So much! They matter to your customers, to your vendors, to that employee's co-workers, to you and every other manager, and these differences have a huge impact on the bottom line. Yes, your employees (of all ages) must have the hard skills to do the job, but the soft skills make all the difference—whether at the lowest end of the technical skill spectrum or the highest.

Of course, some technical skills are in much greater demand and shorter supply—notably in the STEM (science, technology, engineering, and math) fields—mostly because they require a substantial amount of education and training. It's a whole lot more difficult and time-consuming to learn how to be a nurse than it is to learn how to operate a cash register. Employers in health care, computing, software, hardware, accounting, finance, and other "talent wars" industries, need to hire people who have gone to the time and trouble and cost on their own initiative to acquire these in-demand technical skills for these higher-end jobs. That's why these employers are ever scrambling to find enough "qualified" talent. While it's very difficult for these employers to place a real premium on soft skills for very in-demand hard skill jobs, the soft skills are even more important at the high end:

◆ *Even if the nurse got straight A's in nursing school and is great at, say, inserting needles and tubes into the human body, if that nurse falls asleep on the night shift or forgets to note correctly when medicine has been given or does not communicate effectively, then patients will suffer and someone might die.*

◆ *Even if the network systems administrator knows the hardware and software and all the crisscrossing cables, if she fails to do timely updates, or monitor storage capacity, or recognize patterns in user issues, the system might crash and burn.*

◆ *Even if the computer programmer can write great code very fast, if that programmer cannot understand the needs and objectives of business owners/users, that programmer is going to write a lot of great code to nowhere.*

◆ *Even if the data analyst is a master of collection, processing, and reporting, if the analyst doesn't work at a steady pace, becomes distracted easily, and doesn't follow through in a timely manner on key deliverables, the leadership will be starved of key performance indicators and the enterprise could be going down the drain before anybody sees it coming.*

◆ *Even if the engineer can design and develop and test devices of all shapes and sizes, if that engineer refuses to coordinate with other team members by doing the necessary reporting in the project management system; or cuts out early and puts extra work on the rest of the team; or smells bad or sneers or curses at colleagues, there will be stress and conflict on the team.*

◆ *Even if the accountant knows the audit process like the back of her hand, if she does not pay close attention to detail or overlooks details rather than having a difficult conversation or reveals confidential company information on social media, someone could go to jail.*

In our work, I've seen every one of these scenarios played out in the real world. Trust me. Soft skills matter. A lot! They are not trivial. Soft skills make the difference every day between life and death; between success and failure.

Imagine the nurse who not only stays late and takes very few breaks, but whom patients know by name and trust and look forward to seeing; who sees more patients, spends more time with patients, knows more patients by name, and smiles at more patients; notices subtle changes and recognizes important symptoms even when they are not conspicuous; can give a patient or his family a greater feeling of dignity and safety and comfort and motivation—not just medicine.

Here's what's really thrilling: Soft skills can also make the difference between mediocre and good; between good and great; between great and "one of a kind."

Just as I've seen the costly downsides of the soft skills gap, in our work, I've seen example after example proving the incredible power of soft skills. When you combine the necessary hard skills of a job with the right soft skills, the added value is so much more than the sum of its parts. The soft skills are like a supersonic jet fuel that magnifies the scope and quality of every stitch of work.

I promise you, this does not happen by accident.

Drill Down: The Missing Basics

Up to this point, I've been using the term "soft skills," as it is generally understood, to refer to the entire array of non-technical skills. I focus on three old-fashioned categories of soft skills—professionalism, critical thinking, and followership—because they seem like the best way to capture the thousands of details of behavior that managers bring up in our surveys, interviews, focus groups, and seminars. In trying to make them easier to discuss and teach, I've boiled them down to just twelve missing basics and organized them into those three old-fashioned categories:

1. Professionalism: The Missing Basics
♦ *Self-evaluation:* Regularly assessing one's own thoughts, words, and actions against clear meaningful standards and one's own

performance against specific goals, timelines, guidelines, and parameters

♦ *Personal responsibility:* Staying focused on what one can control directly—principally one's self—and controlling one's responses in the face of factors outside one's own control

♦ *Positive attitude:* Maintaining and conveying a positive, generous, enthusiastic demeanor in one's expressions, gestures, words, and tone

♦ *Good work habits:* Wellness, self-presentation, timeliness, organization, productivity, quality, follow-through, and initiative

♦ *People skills:* Attentive listening, observing, and reading; perceiving and empathizing; effective use of words, tone, expressions and gestures—verbal, written, and otherwise—one-on-one and in groups, in-person and remotely

2. Critical Thinking: The Missing Basics

♦ *Proactive learning:* Keeping an open mind, suspending judgment, questioning assumptions, and seeking out information, technique, and perspective, and studying, practicing, and contemplating in order to build one's stored knowledge base, skill set, and wisdom

♦ *Problem solving:* Mastering established best-practices—proven repeatable solutions for dealing with regular recurring decisions—so as to avoid reinventing the wheel. Using repeatable solutions to improvise when addressing decisions that are new but similar

♦ *Decision making:* Identifying and considering multiple options, assessing the pros and cons of each, and choosing the course of action closest to the desired outcome

3. Followership: The Missing Basics

♦ *Respect for context:* Reading and adapting to the existing structure, rules, customs, and leadership in an unfamiliar situation

♦ *Citizenship:* Accepting, embracing, and observing, not just the rights and rewards, but the duties of membership/belonging/participation in a defined group with its own structure, rules, customs, and leadership

◆ *Service:* Approaching relationships in terms of what you have to offer—respect, commitment, hard work, creativity, sacrifice—rather than what you need or want

◆ *Teamwork:* Playing whatever role is needed to support the larger mission; coordinating, cooperating, and collaborating with others in pursuit of a shared goal; supporting and celebrating the success of others

As you read and re-read the descriptions of the missing basics, you should be asking yourself: What are the highest priority behaviors for your organization, for your team, for different roles on your team, and/or for the various individuals on your team? Which behaviors are crucial to success? Which ones offer the greatest potential to increase competitive differentiation?

Imagine the network systems administrator who not only keeps the hardware and software running and updates systems, tracks recurring user issues, finds root causes, and implements systemic solutions to recurring problems—not just maintaining storage, but exploring the cloud or some other innovation; not just a "manager" in title only, but a highly engaged leader who is coaching the other system administrators and technicians on the team.

Unlocking the Power of Soft Skills

Show me an organization with a strong, positive corporate culture and I will show you an organization that is very clear about exactly which soft skill behaviors are high priority and sings about those high priority behaviors from the rooftops often. They don't just focus on their young talent, of course, but their emphasis on key soft skill behaviors makes everybody in the organization much better—even the youngest, least experienced employees. To make it easy for you to picture, I'll ask you to think of the U.S. Marine Corps or picture Disney. Both organizations, in very different lines of work, employ a lot of young people, and both famously imbue a huge number of the soft skill behaviors in their workforce. There are many other examples:

♦ *There is a quick service restaurant chain that stands out as the very best in every single market in which they operate: Their employees, from top to bottom, of all ages, are always super clean-cut, wearing tidy uniforms, prompt and attentive, excessively polite, and always going the extra mile to ensure quality and service. I always jokingly reference "Ned Flanders" from* The Simpsons—*the "goody goody" next door neighbor—when I'm describing the personnel in this organization. Everybody who works there is like "Ned Flanders." The organization is surely not a model of diversity, but it is a model of incredible soft skills throughout the organization. Whether you like Ned Flanders or not, you could see how he would do a great job in a role where what matters most is cleanliness, fresh hot food, and great customer service. Right?*

♦ *On the other end of the spectrum, there is a lunch concession in New York City near Wall Street where everything is made to order—but with lightning speed—that customers must learn to be prepared to order without delay in staccato fashion: "wheat bread, mayonnaise, turkey, muenster cheese, lettuce, tomato, onion," and with barely a pause the guy behind the counter is handing the customer a sandwich wrapped and marked—as the endless line moves swiftly and steadily past a self-service soup selection and beverage refrigerator toward the cashier. If you don't move fast, you miss your opportunities, as the line just keeps moving. Their culture is all about pace (and consistently healthy portions). Customers know exactly what to expect: a very big sandwich, customized 100 percent, and soup and a drink, all very fast. The place is a goldmine.*

♦ *There is a rental car chain that is consistently rated the best and also has been the most profitable and fastest growing for years on end. Why? Self-presentation. Quality. Teamwork. Initiative. Problem solving.*

♦ *There is a health care system where key metrics—wait time in emergency rooms, cost per care incident, safety, patient satisfaction, etc.—far surpass those of comparable hospitals. The reason is their incessant focus on a handful of high priority behaviors among health care delivery personnel: Pace. Quality. Decision Making. Teamwork. Service.*

These powerful corporate cultures don't just happen. They are the result of an organization that knows exactly what its high priority behaviors are, focuses on them relentlessly, and systematically drives those behaviors throughout the organization in all of its human capital management practices. When it works, it really works.

> Imagine the computer programmer who not only writes great code very fast, but also conducts in-depth interviews with business owners/users before, during, and after every key step in the development process, in order to better understand their needs and issues.

To be clear, these organizations do not necessarily use the same terms for key behaviors as they are named and described in our competency model. But if you drill down, you will see the same key soft skill behaviors recurring over and over again, underpinning these powerful cultures.

Most organizations with powerful cultures develop their own poignant language and symbols—slogans and logos—internally and externally. Of course, the best organizations align their employer branding with their branding in the consumer marketplace. Slogans and logos—branding—with compelling messages are an important part of creating the shared meaning in an organization that helps define the culture. But it takes a whole lot more than slogans and logos to drive a powerful culture.

I've worked with some organizations that are all talk and no action when it comes to culture. They have great slogans, but they do not drive and support and reward key behaviors among employees that are in alignment with the messages. When employees have regular run-ins with customers because management has very strict policies against merchandise exchanges and returns, then it really doesn't matter how many placards there are in the store that say, "The customer is always right!" The slogans start to sound pretty empty.

I've also worked with organizations in which the leadership becomes very serious about changing their corporate culture—all of a sudden. It's as if these leaders have an epiphany and realize what they've been missing and decide they want a strong positive culture and they want it now. They want culture change overnight, by decree: "From now on, our culture will be _____!" Fill in the blank—"honesty!" "teamwork!" "innovation!" But you can't force culture change overnight. It takes time because behavior change takes time.

> Imagine the data analyst who not only collects, processes, and reports data in a timely manner, but takes the initiative to report the data in more user-friendly formats so that they are easier to read and understand; to search for important patterns in the data; to extrapolate from those patterns to make meaningful predictions; and has the ability to make an effective verbal presentation to accompany the report.

Of course, there are also plenty of leaders who pay no attention to corporate culture whatsoever. I've had many senior executives tell me: "It was never an issue before these Millennials came along. Employees just did their jobs and behaved like grown-ups. Now that we have this generation gap, we are talking for the first time about our 'culture.'" I always tell these leaders: "Just because you have never paid any attention to culture, doesn't mean you don't have a corporate culture. It just means you have a culture by default instead of by design." Every organization has a corporate culture. Your corporate culture is simply the combined web of prevailing shared beliefs, meaning, language, practices, and traditions that have developed over time between and among the people in your organization.

Take a few minutes to think: How would you describe the culture of your organization? What about your team? Are they aligned? Is your culture by default or design?

> Imagine the engineer who not only designs, develops, and tests devices very well, very fast, but also checks every box on time every step of the way in the project management system; is great at interpersonal communication; actively celebrates the success of others; and is always ready to sacrifice for the team.

Of course, you can't control the whole culture of your entire organization (unless, of course, you are the big, big boss.) Still, whether you are the CEO or a manager with a small team, what you can control is your sphere—whatever part of the organization is your responsibility.

If your organization has a strong positive culture by design, then you need to be in alignment. What are the high priority behaviors? What are you doing in your sphere to drive and support and reward those behaviors in everything you do as a leader?

If your organization has a less than strong positive culture—or a culture by default—then it's all up to you. You need to create your own culture within your own sphere, not just for the young talent, but for everybody. You don't need to start a revolution. But you can be a little bit of a maverick. You can certainly be a change leader. Believe me: Your results will speak for themselves: your team will stand out, not just in its business outcomes, but in cohesiveness, morale, and retention.

What are the high priority behaviors that are most important in your sphere? Crucial to success? Or jet fuel for competitive differentiation? Make them the foundation of your culture. Focus on them relentlessly, and systematically drive those behaviors throughout your sphere in all of your human capital management practices. Develop your own poignant language and symbols—slogans and logos. Make sure it aligns with your organization's "brand." Then sing it from the rooftops. Make it 1,000 percent clear. And start doing everything within your power to drive and support and reward those high priority behaviors in every employee within your sphere.

Imagine the accountant who not only knows the rules, follows the rules, and helps her clients follow the rules, but also has the guts and tact to talk clients through the difficult details and the savvy to help them ethically navigate around, over, under, or through, or maybe even the initiative, creativity, and innovation to find a hidden opportunity or invent the next great loophole.

Unlocking the Power: The Rest of This Book

The rest of this book is dedicated to helping you teach the missing basics—complete with step-by-step lesson plans. Just imagine the impact you could have if you were to spend time every week systematically building up the soft skills of your team. You would send a powerful message, week by week. You would make them aware. You would make them care. You would help them learn the missing basics one by one—one exercise at a time. You would build them up and make them so much better.

PART TWO

HOW TO TEACH THE MISSING BASICS TO TODAY'S YOUNG TALENT

Part Two of this book is dedicated to helping you teach the missing basics—complete with step-by-step lesson plans. The missing basics are organized into chapters based on three old-fashioned categories:

- ◆ How to Teach the Missing Basics of Professionalism
- ◆ How to Teach the Missing Basics of Critical Thinking
- ◆ How to Teach the Missing Basics of Followership

All of the exercises within the lesson plans are exercises we have developed and tested over the years in our "career skills" and "managing your boss" seminars with young people in the workplace, following this basic teaching strategy:

- ◆ *Make them aware:* Name it and describe what the skill means to the organization.
- ◆ *Make them care:* Explore what the skill means to them.
- ◆ *Sell it:* Explain the "self-building" value of the skill.
- ◆ *Break it down:* Spell out exactly what they need to do, step-by-step.
- ◆ *Make it easy:* Use ready-made lessons and exercises.
- ◆ *Involve them:* Give them "credit" for self-directed learning.
- ◆ *Make it practical:* Spotlight opportunities to practice on the job.

◆ Follow up with coaching style feedback to reinforce the lessons whenever possible.

All of the exercises and lessons are designed to be highly flexible and easy to use:

◆ They can be given as "take-home" exercises to any individual or group;
◆ They can be used to guide one-on-one discussions with direct reports;
◆ They can be conducted in a classroom as written exercises or as group discussions;
◆ Almost all of them can be done easily inside of an hour within a team meeting or an extended one-on-one;
◆ Some exercises may be such a good fit for the needs of a particular individual or for your team as a whole that you may find yourself returning to them over and over on a regular basis.

Not every lesson or exercise is for every team or individual, of course. Feel free to modify any of the lessons to fit your needs. Spend time every day or every week building up the soft skills of your team. Send a powerful message. Make them aware. Make them care. Help them learn the missing basics one by one—one exercise at a time. Build them up and make them better. They will be so glad you did. You will be, too! Not to mention every manager they ever have for the rest of their careers.

Chapter 4

How to Teach the Missing Basics of Professionalism to Today's Young Talent

Professionalism: The Missing Basics

Self-evaluation: Regularly assessing one's own thoughts, words, and actions against clear, meaningful standards; and one's own performance against specific goals, timelines, guidelines, and parameters.

Personal responsibility: Staying focused on what one can control directly—principally one's self—and controlling one's responses in the face of factors outside one's own control.

Positive attitude: Maintaining and conveying a positive, generous, enthusiastic demeanor in one's expressions, gestures, words, and tone.

Good work habits: Wellness, self-presentation, timeliness, organization, productivity, quality, follow-through, and initiative.

People skills: Attentive listening, observing, and reading; perceiving and empathizing; effective use of words, tone, expressions, and gestures—verbal, written, and otherwise; one-on-one and in groups; in-person and remotely.

How to Teach Self-Evaluation

Self-evaluation: Regularly assessing one's own thoughts, words, and actions against clear, meaningful standards, and one's own performance against specific goals, timelines, guidelines, and parameters.

THE GAP

> *Manager:* "For goodness sake, these young upstarts need to take a step back and get a reality check. I want to say, 'Take a look in the mirror!'"
>
> *Gen Z:* "I like what I see!"

THE BRIDGE: WHAT YOU, THE MANAGER, NEED TO REMEMBER

Here is a profound truth I learned from my longtime karate teacher, mentor and friend Master Frank Gorman: "The mirror is the best teacher."

That is not true, however, if you always like what you see. I don't mean this to seem like a retro anti-self-esteem movement "make-a-point" moment. But if you always like what you see in the mirror, then you are actually a per se narcissist. In order to use the mirror as a teacher, one must have an external objective standard against which to measure one's reflection. I'm not talking about artistic beauty or saying one kind of reflection is "better" than another in any kind of absolute way. Even if you make up the objective standard yourself, the key is using that standard to measure future performance. Juxtaposition with a clear standard is a necessary component of any kind of productive evaluation—especially self-evaluation. Otherwise, self-evaluation turns into navel gazing—solipsism—which is distorting due to narrowing perspective and therefore leads straight to unconditional self-acceptance or paralyzing self-loathing. Neither drives learning and growth.

What does drive learning and growth?

Regular, productive, honest self-evaluation against clear standards. That is not only the fundamental building block for teaching/learning the rest of the self-management skills, but is the fundamental building block for teaching/learning all of the soft skills, not to mention every hard skill. Not to mention practically any other kind of significant learning and growth. When it comes to continuous improvement of any kind, self-evaluation is the beginning, middle, and end.

For that reason, most of the lesson plans and exercises throughout the rest of this book revolve around self-evaluation tools of various types. Before you get into the lesson plans here, you might consider starting with some big picture assessment tools—tools that profile personality types, interests, values, and/or communication style. Try to identify (and vet) several of them—the more the better.

Where can you find them? Your organization may own some already. Ask someone in HR. Or you can look online. You can find many free and plenty more for sale. You can find them in books. You can often find a consultant who will be happy to help. Or you can create one yourself without too much trouble, based on any competency model or any list of traits, characteristics, behaviors, skills, or preferences.

There is an endless supply of reasonably easy to access off-the shelf tools, including:

- ◆ Probably the best-known personality profiling tool is the Myers-Briggs Type Indicator, which is a proprietary tool that separates people into sixteen types based on how they take in information, how they make decisions, whether they draw energy from internal sources or external, and whether they prefer to keep issues open or move them toward closure.
- ◆ Another personality profile I like very much—a model on what I would call the "groovy" end of the spectrum—is called the "Enneagram," which separates people into nine categories based on differences in what ultimately motivates a person on the deepest level.
- ◆ In the middle of the spectrum are many very interesting profiles of communication styles using different frameworks of evaluation: direct/indirect, rational/emotional, assertive/receptive, aggressive/passive/passive-aggressive/manipulative.

Most can now be done online with automated reporting. Or you can often print out an assessment (or buy a kit) so it can be filled out on paper with an old-fashioned pen. Some are best delivered verbally with an "interviewer."

You don't have to choose which big-picture assessment tool is best because you should have them do several different self-assessments, using several different models. Finding one's "type" according to multiple different models is a great way to obtaining multiple perspectives on one's self in very short order.

Do several of them. One option is to take them one at a time. Have your Gen Zers complete a different self-assessment tool every two weeks. In the intervening two weeks between assessments, ask them to really digest the results. The second option is to take them through a self-assessment "boot camp" by completing a series of self-assessments in a very short timeframe. Either way, just the process of completing a self-evaluation tool usually has a significant impact and, of course, the results are usually quite illuminating, especially when one has the results from multiple models to consider. Using the results as a tool for one-on-one coaching will take it to a higher level still. Try to use their individual results as a springboard to provide some coaching style feedback along the way.

For Gen Zers in particular, this is a very powerful lesson because it helps them put specific language around what makes them "different" and where they fit in relation to others. You'll also show them that they actually have a whole lot in common with a whole lot of people. They are often surprised that they can be described as a recognizable type. That will give them a huge dose of self-awareness in a very short period of time.

These tools are a great shortcut to jump-start anybody's path to greater self-awareness. The downside of these tools is they usually take for granted that one's type is fixed; the idea is "this is who you are" and that's not going to change. That's one reason I so strongly advocate using several different models so at least they gain a wider perspective on who they are.

Once you help Gen Zers become familiar and comfortable with self-assessments, they might find they like them. If they really catch the bug, there is a good chance they will go online and find any number of self-evaluations that are more (or less) to their liking. You might even consider assigning them to go online and do some self-directed learning by finding a number of self-evaluation tools, trying them out, and letting you know which ones they think are best. Over time, you will build up a considerable catalogue of these tools. Have them self-evaluate by measuring everything . . . at least everything that matters.

More and more organizations are integrating into their cultures a regular practice of "measuring." The question is: What are they in the habit of measuring? Too often, what is measured most is removed from what individuals feel they can actually control. So the "numbers" they are always hearing about don't tell them very much about their own performance and how they themselves can specifically improve. When it comes to using self-awareness to drive continuous improvement, the key is measuring concrete actions within the control of the individual.

Once your Gen Zers are in the habit of regular self-evaluation, take it to the next level by having them start measuring the concrete actions within their own control—the ones that matter—every step of the way.

In other words, teach them to keep score for themselves on everything they actually do at work. Help them create their own self-evaluation tools to monitor, measure, and document everything they do:

- For every project, there should be a project plan, including every goal and deadline along the way, complete with guidelines and parameters for every goal. Why not teach Gen Zers to use project plans as tools for ongoing self-evaluation? Every step of the way, they can track where they are on every goal.
- For every recurring task or responsibility, there should be standard operating procedures, complete with checklists. Why not teach Gen Zers to use those standard operating procedures and checklists as tools for ongoing self-evaluation? Every step of the way, they can track their progress on every task, one "check" at a time.
- To measure activities, log every activity.
- To measure time, create schedules and time logs.

If they learn and develop habits of using these kinds of self-evaluation tools to monitor their own performance—measuring their own concrete actions against clear, measurable goals—you will put them squarely on the path to continuous improvement. These tools also give you a great way to provide ongoing guidance, direction, support, and coaching about their ongoing work. Their scorekeeping will double as a great source of ongoing real-time documentation.

TEACHING/LEARNING OBJECTIVE

Help your Gen Zers create the habits of regular, productive, honest self-evaluation against meaningful external standards.

MAKE THEM AWARE/MAKE THEM CARE

Your script: "This is why you should really care about creating the habit of regular self-evaluation: Research studies show that what really drives learning and growth is real self-awareness through regular, productive, honest self-evaluation against clear standards. That is the fundamental building block for systematically learning any skill. Without measuring yourself against some measuring stick, it is very hard to set meaningful, concrete goals for improvement, much less monitor your progress on the way toward meeting those goals. If you want to run far, you should measure your distance. If you want to run fast, you should measure your distance over time. If you want to run smarter, you should measure your training regimen against established best practices. If you want to run for charity, then you need to measure how much money you raise. And so on.

"The key is to get into the habit of doing regular self-evaluation against external standards to build greater self-awareness in yourself so you can support your own learning and growth going forward. Remember, 'The mirror is the best teacher,' provided that you learn how to use the mirror to measure your own performance against concrete goals for improvement."

Self–Evaluation: Lesson Plan 1—Introduction

Step One   *Brainstorm:* What does "self-evaluation" mean to you?

Step Two   Consider the following definition of "self-evaluation":

- "Regularly assessing one's own thoughts, words, and actions against clear, meaningful standards, and one's own performance against specific goals, timelines, guidelines, and parameters."

Brainstorm: Why is this approach in the best interests of the organization? Why is this approach in your best interests as an employee? Why is that the key to self-evaluation?

Step Three   Can you think of examples of individuals—inside or outside of work—exemplifying this approach to regular self-evaluation? Can you describe the example in detail? What happened? Where? When? Who was involved?

Step Four   Can you think of examples of a time when you exemplified this approach to regular self-evaluation—inside or outside of work? Can you describe the example in detail? What happened? Where? When? Who else was involved?

Self-Evaluation: Lesson Plan 2—Evaluating Yourself on Ability, Skill, and Will

Evaluate yourself, generally, in terms of your natural abilities, skills, and motivation.

Ability

- ◆ What are my natural strengths that are applicable to my current tasks and responsibilities and projects? How am I applying those strengths?
- ◆ What are my relative weaknesses? How can I better leverage my strengths? How can I better plan around, bolster, or otherwise mitigate my weaknesses?

Technical Skills

- ◆ What are my key technical skills applicable to my current tasks and responsibilities and projects? How am I applying those skills?
- ◆ What are my relative technical skill gaps? How can I better leverage my skills? How can I bridge those skill gaps?

Soft Skills

- ◆ What are my key soft skills applicable to my current tasks and responsibilities and projects? How am I applying those skills?
- ◆ What are my relative soft skill gaps? How can I better leverage my soft skills? How can I bridge those soft skill gaps?

Will/Motivation

- ◆ What is my current motivation level? High, medium, or low?
- ◆ In what areas inside or outside of work am I most motivated?
- ◆ What motivates me? What can I do to find more of what motivates me?
- ◆ What demotivates me? What can I do to avoid those things that demotivate me?

Self-Evaluation: Lesson Plan 3—Evaluating Yourself on Productivity, Quality, and Behavior

Evaluate yourself generally in terms of the major dimensions of performance at work.

Productivity
◆ Are you doing enough work fast enough?
◆ What can you do to get more work done faster?
◆ Should you revisit your priorities?
◆ Do you need to focus your time better?
◆ Do you need to postpone low-priority activities?
◆ How can you eliminate time-wasters?
◆ Do you need better time budgets?
◆ Do you need to make better plans?

Quality
◆ Are you meeting or exceeding guidelines and specifications for your tasks and responsibilities?
◆ What can you do to improve the quality of your work?
◆ Do you need to pay closer attention to detail?
◆ Do you need to make better use of checklists?
◆ Do you need to start adding some bells and whistles to your work product?

Behavior
◆ What can you do to make sure that your intangible behaviors are positive?
◆ Are there substandard behaviors you can eliminate? Which ones? How can you eliminate them?
◆ Are there superstar behaviors you can add? How can you add them?
◆ Should you be taking more initiative or less?
◆ How can you take more initiative without overstepping your bounds?

Self-Evaluation: Lesson Plan 4—Evaluating Yourself on the Key Soft Skills Competencies

Complete the following self-evaluation based on our soft skills competency model. For each, answer the following questions:

When it comes to your natural abilities and inclinations:
- Is this a natural strength? Or is this a natural weakness?
- On a scale of 1 (weakest) to 10 (strongest)

When it comes to your learned skills:
- Is this a skill you've practiced and made strong? Or is this a weakness?
- On a scale of 1 (weakest) to 10 (strongest)

When it comes to your experience:
- Is this a skill in which you have gained a lot of experience? Or very little?
- On a scale of 1 (no experience) to 10 (extensive experience)

When it comes to your interest and motivation:
- Is this a skill in which you are interested and motivated:
- On a scale of 1 (not interested) to 10 (extremely motivated)

THE BASICS OF PROFESSIONALISM

The soft skill of *Self-Evaluation*: Regularly assessing one's own thoughts, words, and actions against clear meaningful standards, and one's own performance against specific goals, timelines, guidelines, and parameters.

The soft skill of *Personal Responsibility*: Staying focused on what one can control directly—principally one's self—and controlling one's responses in the face of factors outside one's own control.

The soft skill of *Positive Attitude*: Maintaining and conveying a positive, generous, enthusiastic demeanor in one's expressions, gestures, words, and tone.

The soft skill of *Good Work Habits*: Wellness, self-presentation, timeliness, organization, productivity, quality, follow-through, and initiative.

The soft skill of *People Skills*: Attentive listening, observing, and reading; perceiving and empathizing; effective use of words, tone, expressions, and gestures—verbal, written, and otherwise—one-on-one and in groups; in person, and remotely.

THE BASICS OF CRITICAL THINKING

The soft skill of *Proactive Learning*: Keeping an open mind, suspending judgment, questioning assumptions, and seeking out information, technique, and perspective, and studying, practicing, and contemplating in order to build one's stored knowledge base, skill-set, and wisdom.

The soft skill of *Problem Solving*: Mastering established best-practices—proven repeatable solutions for dealing with regular recurring decisions—so as to avoid reinventing the wheel. Using repeatable solutions to improvise when addressing decisions that are new but similar.

The soft skill of *Decision Making*: Identifying and considering multiple options, assessing the pros and cons of each, and choosing the course of action closest to the desired outcome.

THE BASICS OF FOLLOWERSHIP

The soft skill of *Respect for Context*: Reading and adapting to the existing structure, rules, customs, and leadership in an unfamiliar situation.

The soft skill of *Good Citizenship*: Accepting, embracing, and observing, not just the rights and rewards, but the duties of membership/belonging/participation in a defined group with its own structure, rules, customs, and leadership.

The soft skill of *Service*: Approaching relationships in terms of what you have to offer—respect, commitment, hard work, creativity, sacrifice—rather than what you need or want.

The soft skill of *Teamwork*: Playing whatever role is needed to support the larger mission; coordinating, cooperating, and collaborating with others in pursuit of a shared goal; supporting and celebrating the success of others.

Self–Evaluation: Lesson Plan 5—Drill Down on Understanding the Key Soft Skills

Complete the following self-evaluation based on our soft skills competency model.

Answer the following questions for each soft skill below:

◆ Can you think of a person you believe to be highly effective at this skill?

◆ Can you think of an example you've witnessed of this skill in action? Can you describe it? What makes this skill in action so valuable? What can you learn from this?

THE BASICS OF PROFESSIONALISM

The soft skill of *Self-Evaluation*: Regularly assessing one's own thoughts, words, and actions against clear meaningful standards, and one's own performance against specific goals, timelines, guidelines, and parameters.

The soft skill of *Personal Responsibility*: Staying focused on what one can control directly—principally one's self—and controlling one's responses in the face of factors outside one's own control.

The soft skill of *Positive Attitude*: Maintaining and conveying a positive, generous, enthusiastic demeanor in one's expressions, gestures, words, and tone.

The soft skill of *Good Work Habits*: Wellness, self-presentation, timeliness, organization, productivity, quality, follow-through, and initiative.

The soft skill of *People Skills*: Attentive listening, observing, and reading; perceiving and empathizing; effective use of words, tone, expressions, and gestures—verbal, written, and otherwise—one-on-one and in groups; in person, and remotely.

THE BASICS OF CRITICAL THINKING

The soft skill of *Proactive Learning*: Keeping an open mind, suspending judgment, questioning assumptions, and seeking out information, technique, and perspective, and studying, practicing, and contemplating in order to build one's stored knowledge base, skill-set, and wisdom.

The soft skill of *Problem Solving*: Mastering established best-practices—proven repeatable solutions for dealing with regular recurring decisions—so as to avoid reinventing the wheel. Using repeatable solutions to improvise when addressing decisions that are new but similar.

The soft skill of *Decision Making*: Identifying and considering multiple options, assessing the pros and cons of each, and choosing the course of action closest to the desired outcome.

THE BASICS OF FOLLOWERSHIP

The soft skill of *Respect for Context*: Reading and adapting to the existing structure, rules, customs, and leadership in an unfamiliar situation.

The soft skill of *Good Citizenship*: Accepting, embracing, and observing, not just the rights and rewards, but the duties of membership/belonging/participation in a defined group with its own structure, rules, customs, and leadership.

The soft skill of *Service*: Approaching relationships in terms of what you have to offer—respect, commitment, hard work, creativity, sacrifice—rather than what you need or want.

The soft skill of *Teamwork*: Playing whatever role is needed to support the larger mission; coordinating, cooperating, and collaborating with others in pursuit of a shared goal; supporting and celebrating the success of others.

Self-Evaluation: Lesson Plan 6—Explore Your Own Successes with the Key Soft Skills

Complete the following self-evaluation based on our soft skills competency model.

Answer the following questions for each of the skills:

◆ Can you think of a time when you've been successful with this skill in action? Can you describe what happened? What happened? When? Where? Who else was involved? What lessons did you take away from this experience?

◆ How could you improve when it comes to this skill? What are your goals for improvement? What resources are available to you? What support do you need? What is your plan? What is your next step?

THE BASICS OF PROFESSIONALISM

The soft skill of *Self-Evaluation*: Regularly assessing one's own thoughts, words, and actions against clear meaningful standards, and one's own performance against specific goals, timelines, guidelines, and parameters.

The soft skill of *Personal Responsibility*: Staying focused on what one can control directly—principally one's self—and controlling one's responses in the face of factors outside one's own control.

The soft skill of *Positive Attitude*: Maintaining and conveying a positive, generous, enthusiastic demeanor in one's expressions, gestures, words, and tone.

The soft skill of *Good Work Habits*: Wellness, self-presentation, timeliness, organization, productivity, quality, follow-through, and initiative.

The soft skill of *People Skills*: Attentive listening, observing, and reading; perceiving and empathizing; effective use of words, tone, expressions, and gestures—verbal, written, and otherwise—one-on-one and in groups; in person, and remotely.

THE BASICS OF CRITICAL THINKING

The soft skill of *Proactive Learning*: Keeping an open mind, suspending judgment, questioning assumptions, and seeking out information, technique, and perspective, and studying, practicing, and contemplating in order to build one's stored knowledge base, skill-set, and wisdom.

The soft skill of *Problem Solving*: Mastering established best-practices—proven repeatable solutions for dealing with regular recurring decisions—so as to avoid reinventing the wheel. Using repeatable solutions to improvise when addressing decisions that are new but similar.

The soft skill of *Decision Making*: Identifying and considering multiple options, assessing the pros and cons of each, and choosing the course of action closest to the desired outcome.

THE BASICS OF FOLLOWERSHIP

The soft skill of *Respect for Context*: Reading and adapting to the existing structure, rules, customs, and leadership in an unfamiliar situation.

The soft skill of *Good Citizenship*: Accepting, embracing, and observing, not just the rights and rewards, but the duties of membership/belonging/participation in a defined group with its own structure, rules, customs, and leadership.

The soft skill of *Service*: Approaching relationships in terms of what you have to offer—respect, commitment, hard work, creativity, sacrifice—rather than what you need or want.

The soft skill of *Teamwork*: Playing whatever role is needed to support the larger mission; coordinating, cooperating, and collaborating with others in pursuit of a shared goal; supporting and celebrating the success of others.

How to Teach Personal Responsibility

Personal responsibility: Staying focused on what one can control directly—principally one's own thoughts, words, and actions—and controlling one's responses in the face of factors outside one's own control.

THE GAP

> *Manager:* "They are too quick to make excuses for themselves, blame others, and complain about external influences, obstacles, and constraints."
>
> *Gen Z:* "In my entry-level position, I often feel powerless in the face of so many factors outside my control."

THE BRIDGE: WHAT YOU, THE MANAGER, MUST REMEMBER

Here is the reality: In any situation, there are factors beyond our control. For example, I feel gravity and time are constantly holding me back! And in any situation there are factors within our control: our own thoughts, words, and actions. Almost anyone can focus on those outside factors or those inside factors. In fact, there is a lot of evidence to suggest that most people—of all ages—have a tendency to point to outside factors beyond their control when explaining their own shortcomings and failures, not to mention the successes of others. Funny enough, most people also have a strong tendency to point to factors within the direct control of the individual when it comes to our own successes as well as the failures and shortcomings of others. So the good news is that most people know how to focus on factors within their control. It's just that we take our focus off those factors when we make excuses, blame others, and complain.

When it comes to teaching personal responsibility, the key is keeping the focus on factors within the control of the individual—teaching people to ask themselves every step of the way: What is within my control right now? Where will I focus my attention and energy? What are my options? What's the plan? What are my next steps? What are my next thoughts, words, and actions?

TEACHING/LEARNING OBJECTIVE

Help your Gen Zers take greater personal responsibility by learning to stay focused on concrete actions within their own control.

MAKE THEM AWARE/MAKE THEM CARE

Your script: "This is why you should really care about increasing your sense of personal responsibility: No matter how high or how low your position, if you focus your attention and energy on factors outside your control, you will render yourself 'powerless,' by definition. However, the flip side is also true. No matter how high or how low your position, if you focus your attention and energy on factors within your control, you will maximize your power. In any situation, no matter how little is within your control, the way to make yourself more powerful is to focus like a laser beam on whatever thoughts, words, and actions you *can* take—your choices and the effects you can cause. Sometimes it is a very small amount of power, but more power is better than less power.

"The key is learning to ask yourself every step of the way: 'What is within my control right now? Where will I focus my attention and energy? What are my options? What's the plan? What are my next steps? What are my next thoughts, words, and actions?' That's how you increase your 'response power' in any situation."

Personal Responsibility: Lesson Plan 1—Introduction

Step One *Brainstorm:* What does "personal responsibility" mean to you?

Step Two Consider the following definition of "personal responsibility": "Staying focused on what one can control directly—principally one's own thoughts, words, and actions—and controlling one's responses in the face of factors outside one's own control." Brainstorm: Why is this approach to personal responsibility in the best interests of the organization? Why is this approach to personal responsibility in your best interests as an employee? Why is that the key to personal responsibility?

Step Three Can you think of examples of individuals—inside or outside of work—exemplifying this approach to personal responsibility? Can you describe the example in detail? What happened? Where? When? Who was involved?

Step Four Can you think of examples of a time when you exemplified this approach to personal responsibility—inside or outside of work? Can you describe the example in detail? What happened? Where? When? Who else was involved?

Personal Responsibility: Lesson Plan 2—All the Factors That Are in Your Way

Step One   Brainstorm all of the factors that get in the way of your ability to do your job and make it harder for you to perform at the highest level.

Step Two   Now take a look at all the factors you've listed and ask yourself, for each factor: "Is this a factor within my control or outside my control?" Take note of how many are within and how many are outside your control. What is the score?

Step Three   Consider the factors, one by one. For each:

1. Can you think of a recent example? Exactly how did this factor get in your way? When? Where? Who was involved? What happened?
2. What did you do? What could you have done differently, in retrospect? What were your options? What thoughts, words, and actions could you have taken?
3. Now look ahead: Can you anticipate this factor getting in your way in the future? When is that likely to happen? Where? Who might be involved? What do you think is likely to happen? How will you respond? What options will you have? What thoughts, words, and/or actions are available to you? What can you do to improve the outcome?

Personal Responsibility: Lesson Plan 3—Considering the Most Common Factors That Get in the Way at Work

Step One Consider the following factors that people in the workplace commonly list when asked to brainstorm factors that get in their way at work.

- Resource constraints—insufficient information, people, material, or tools
- Limited time
- Too much work
- Other people not doing their part
- Things are constantly changing
- Competing priorities
- Distance
- Weather
- Company policies, rules, regulations, and procedures
- The way things have always been done around here
- Too many low priority distractions
- Interruptions
- Conflict between and among employees
- Manager is often unavailable
- Unclear lines of authority
- Answering to too many different people
- Inconsistency from one manager to another

Step Three Consider the factors above, one by one. For each:

1. Can you think of a recent example? Exactly how did this factor get in your way? When? Where? Who was involved? What happened?
2. Ask yourself: What did you do? What could you have done differently, in retrospect? What were your options? What thoughts, words, and actions could you have taken?
3. Now look ahead: Can you anticipate this factor getting in your way in the future? When is that likely to happen? Where? Who might be involved? What do you think is likely to happen? How will you respond? What options will you have? What thoughts, words, and/or actions are available to you? What can you do to improve the outcome?

Personal Responsibility: Lesson Plan 4—Response Power

Step One   Learn to use the "response power" mantra. Focus on the list of problems/obstacles that get in your way at work. Now take those items on your list, one by one, and practice applying the "response power" mantra: "What's outside my control? What's inside my control? (My own thoughts, words, actions) What are my options? What are my next steps?"

Step Two   Learn to use this simple tool to go along with the "response power" mantra.

For any situation, simply arrange those questions in a horizontal axis at the top of a page to make vertical columns, and then fill in your answers side by side.

Outside	Inside (My Own Thoughts, Words, Actions)	Options?	Next Steps

Step Three   Practice using the mantra and tool.

- ◆ Choose a factor outside your control that you can anticipate being in your way in the near future.
- ◆ Now apply the mantra and the tool to think through in advance and prepare. Ask yourself:
  - • What's outside my control?
  - • What's inside my control (my own thoughts, words, actions)?
  - • What are my options?
  - • What are my next steps?"

Step Four   Consider the question, "What about those times when there really is nothing you can do?"

Consider the following: If there is really nothing you can do, then why are you still thinking about it? Why are you still talking about it? Focus on something you CAN do.

Step Five   HOMEWORK. Use "response power"—the mantra and the tool—whenever it is appropriate going forward. Discuss it with your manager in your one-on-ones.

How to Teach Positive Attitude

Positive attitude: Conveying optimism, generosity, support, and enthusiasm in one's expressions, gestures, words, and tone.

THE GAP

> *Manager:* "Whether it is positive or negative, they feel like they need to share their feelings. This whole generation needs an attitude adjustment. Or at least just 'keep it to yourself.'"
>
> *Gen Zer:* "Hey, sorry, I gotta be me. That's just who I am. I do my job. Why should they care what I'm thinking or feeling on the inside?"

THE BRIDGE: WHAT YOU, THE MANAGER, NEED TO REMEMBER

There is no doubt, employee attitudes affect productivity, quality, morale; collegiality, cooperation, and cohesion; employee development; and retention, as well as turnover. Good employee attitudes drive positive results. Bad employee attitudes put a drag on results. That's a fact proven by study after study, including our own.

Do Gen Zers really need a generation-wide attitude adjustment? Perhaps they've all been conditioned by social media to err on the side of over-sharing. Maybe so, but even if you could get inside their heads, you shouldn't try. It is not your job to be your employees' therapist. What you must do instead is focus on the external behavior. What they can do, for sure, is learn to keep their negative feelings to themselves and "smile on the outside" more at work.

Do not make the three most common mistakes that most managers make when dealing with "bad attitudes":

♦ Treating attitude as a personal issue, an "internal" state of mind that is off limits
♦ Treating attitude as unchangeable ("that's just who I am") matter of personality
♦ Talking about attitude in vague terms or indirectly

As long as you think of attitude as a personal, internal matter, it is going to remain intangible and you will remain out of your depth. Feelings are on the inside. Observable behavior is on the outside.

That observable behavior can be seen, heard, and felt. No matter how intrinsic the source may be, only the external behavior can be and must be managed. As a leader, dealing with attitude becomes a whole lot easier if you treat it head-on, directly, as just another matter of performance management. Here's my best advice:

- Make great attitude an explicit and regularly discussed performance requirement for everyone.
- Make it about external behaviors, which employees can modify as necessary.
- Define the behaviors of great attitude: expressions, words, tone, and gestures. Describe the behaviors. Require them. Teach them. Reward people for displaying them proudly. Hold people accountable when they don't.

LEARNING OBJECTIVE

Help Gen Zers to focus on conveying optimism, generosity, support, and enthusiasm in their external attitude behaviors—their expressions, words, tone, and gestures.

MAKE THEM AWARE/MAKE THEM CARE

Your script: "This is why you should care about demonstrating a positive attitude at work: Attitude may be hard to define and describe— great, good, bad, or average. But it is very, very important. At every level, leaders and managers rate 'attitude' as one of the most important factors in employee performance. Attitude can be the difference between success and failure for our business. Attitude can be the difference between success and failure for any employee.

"Even so, many leaders and managers fail to talk about the power of attitude. Many believe that attitude is a personal issue, so it is off limits. Many believe that attitude is just 'who a person is' and can't be changed, so they don't try. Many believe attitude is vague, so they wouldn't know where to begin. Those beliefs are all wrong, and that approach is a big mistake.

"Here's the good news: Attitude is not a vague internal matter that is unchangeable. Like anything else, displaying a positive attitude is a skill set that can be learned and mastered. Attitude is simply too important to leave off the table. So we are going to talk about it. We are going to focus on external behaviors. The bottom line is simple: Good attitudes are required. Not on the inside. What you feel on the inside is your business, 100 percent. But on the outside, positive words, tones, and gestures are required and expected. Here's some more good news: Research shows that if you make an effort to display positive words, tones, and gestures on the outside, it has a positive effect on your internal brain chemistry and it actually makes you feel better on the inside.

"Here's the bottom line: If you learn to display a positive attitude at work, regardless of what you are feeling inside, then you will have learned one of the most important broad transferable skills you could ever learn. You will be valued for your positive attitude in any role in any organization anywhere any time. And that is a skill that will never become obsolete."

Positive Attitude: Lesson Plan 1—Considering Theories of How to Be Your Best at Work

There are a lot of theories out there about how to bring out the best attitudes in people at work. Consider the leading ideas:

- *Idea 1. Play to your strengths at work*: Work primarily on tasks and responsibilities that you enjoy and are particularly good at. The only problem is that most of us don't have that luxury.
  - *Brainstorming Question:* How do you keep doing good work day after day—and feel good about it—when the work is not necessarily work that you enjoy or excel at?
- *Idea 2. Balance your time at work with free time:* Rest, recover, relax, and rejuvenate in between times you must work. But the problem is that most of us simply don't have enough time to do everything we need to do each day, much less have "free" time.
  - *Brainstorming Question:* How do you stay focused and energetic when you barely have time to think, much less rest?
- *Idea 3. Work with people you like and respect:* Avoid people you find "toxic" and stick to the ones you appreciate. The only problem is that very few people can choose their co-workers, subordinates, bosses, vendors, and customers.
  - *Brainstorming Question:* How do you maintain your equilibrium and equanimity when you have to deal with so many people whom you probably would not choose as your colleagues?
- *Idea 4. Work in a workspace that is comfortable and in a location that you enjoy.* If only!
  - *Brainstorming Question:* How do you stay upbeat and strong if you are physically uncomfortable at work or stuck in a location that is not your preference?
- *Idea 5. Leave your non-work issues at the door when you arrive at work.* The problem is: If things are adrift in your life outside of work, then you will be distracted by those concerns, whether you are at work or at home.
  - *Brainstorming Question:* How can you remain focused and positive at work when things might be problematic in your personal life?

Positive Attitude: Lesson Plan 2—Defining "Good Attitude" Behaviors with Your Team—or Any Individual

Step One   Make a list: What does it mean to have a great attitude? Make a list of as many traits, characteristics, and behaviors as you possibly can.

Step Two   Take the first item on your "good attitude" list. Break it down. Spell it out. Describe it. Describe it. Describe it some more.

Step Three   Take the remaining items on your "good attitude" list, one by one, and repeat the process above. Break it down. Spell it out. Describe, describe, describe.

Step Four   Consider your detailed descriptions of "good attitude" traits, characteristics, and behaviors. What are the recurring external behaviors you can identify? What are the recurring expressions, words, tones, and gestures?

Step Five   Considering the above: How would you define "good attitude" in terms of observable measurable external behaviors?

Step Six   Consider: Are these behaviors that can be made performance requirements? If so, how?

Positive Attitude: Lesson Plan 3—Considering Common Bad Attitudes

This is a simple self-evaluation tool to help your employees identify their own weaknesses when it comes to attitude. The following questionnaire is based on our research on the most common aberrant communication practices in the workplace, otherwise known as "bad attitudes."

Everybody has bad days or bad moments. The purpose of this exercise is not to find out whether or not you have a bad attitude. The purpose is to figure out—when you do have bad days or bad moments—what kind of bad attitude behavior are you most likely to display? Armed with that information, you will be much better prepared to avoid that behavior and take corrective action more swiftly when it does happen.

Do you sometimes behave like a "porcupine"?
- Porcupines send the message: "Get away from me!"

Do you sometimes behave like an "entangler"?
- Entanglers want everybody else to be involved in their issues. They want to be noticed, observed, listened to, and engaged, even if their issues are not the concern of the other person.

Do you sometimes behave like a "debater"?
- Debaters always have an argument to make, regardless of whether it is a good argument or not.

Do you sometimes behave like a "complainer"?
- Complainers point out the negatives of a situation without offering a solution that addresses the root cause.

Do you sometimes behave like a "blamer"?
- Blamers are like complainers, pointing out negatives, but blamers point the finger at others or a specific individual.

Do you sometimes behave like a "stink bomb thrower"?
- Stink bomb throwers make sarcastic (or worse) remarks, curse under their breath (or aloud), or even make loud gestures such as slamming things or yelling.

Which bad attitude behaviors are you most likely to display? What does it look like when you display those behaviors? Specifically describe your behavior in those circumstances. What can you do to avoid behaving that way in the future? What can you do to stop yourself when you catch yourself behaving that way in the future?

Positive Attitude: Lesson Plan 4—Considering Good Attitude Behaviors

This is a simple self-evaluation tool to help your employees identify their own strengths when it comes to attitude. The following questionnaire is based on our research on the most highly valued communication practices in the workplace, otherwise known as "good attitudes."

Even if you have bad moments or bad days, you have plenty of good attitude in you. Everybody does. The purpose of this exercise is not to find out whether or not you have a good attitude. The purpose is to figure out—when you are at your best—what kinds of good attitude behaviors you most often display. Armed with that information, you can try to leverage that strength. Not only that, but you may become aware of other "good attitude" behaviors you would like to add to your repertoire!

◆ When you are at your best, are you approachable, welcoming, and professional?

◆ When you are at your best, do you communicate in a highly purposeful manner—brief, straightforward, and efficient?

◆ When you are at your best, do you choose your arguments carefully and make your arguments based on clear evidence, rather than assertions of opinion?

◆ When you are at your best, are you a troubleshooter, placing the focus on what steps you can take yourself to make things better?

◆ When you are at your best, do you go out of your way to make positive, optimistic, generous comments? Speak in positive tones? Make positive gestures and expressions?

Which good attitude behaviors are you most likely to display? What does it look like when you display those behaviors? Specifically describe your behavior in those circumstances. What can you do to leverage those strengths more in the future? What can you do to display other positive behaviors and leverage them as well?

Positive Attitude: Lesson Plan 5—For Individual Employees Who Need an Attitude Adjustment

With all of your direct reports, reinforce the importance of good attitude behaviors in your regular team meetings and one-on-one dialogues as a regular part of your ongoing guidance, direction, support, and coaching.

When an employee starts to behave like someone with a "bad attitude," you need to really zero in on the issue.

Step One   Describe the specific words, tone, and gestures observed.

Step Two   Connect the behavior to concrete work outcomes.

Step Three   Make reference to the performance requirement or best practice from which the negative behavior deviates.

Step Four   Define the replacement behavior that you will use as a specific performance expectation against which to measure the individual's improvement.

Step Five   Continue to follow up in your ongoing one-on-ones. Pay attention. Monitor, measure, and document as best you can. Ask the individual to self-monitor and report to you on progress on a regular basis. Reward success. Do not accept failure.

How to Teach Good Work Habits

Good work habits: Self-presentation, timeliness, organization, productivity, quality, follow-through, consistency, and initiative.

THE GAP

> *Manager:* "These are all things we used to take for granted: Taking care of yourself outside of work so you come in on time ready to work; grooming and dressing appropriately; saying 'please' and 'thank you'; keeping yourself organized and getting your work done consistently. Nobody had to tell me any of that when I was young. In a first job, we would have thought there was something terribly wrong with someone if we had to tell him any of that stuff."

> *Gen Zer:* "I honestly cannot believe they really care about that stuff! You really care if I come in at 8:15 instead of 8?! You really care if I shave?! You have opinions about what I wear?! One of the partners told me, 'Don't come in to my office unless you are prepared to take notes.' I was like, 'Don't even . . .' you know? Like 'Back off . . . don't take yourself so seriously.'"

THE BRIDGE: WHAT YOU, THE MANAGER, NEED TO REMEMBER

Basic work habits are matters of "self-management," which has been a recurring theme in our work nearly since our research began. That's because 99 percent of managers I've ever met would rather not have to do all the hard work of managing their direct reports, but instead deal with employees who pretty much manage themselves: "Do everything they are supposed to do when and how they are supposed to do it, on their own, without guidance, direction, or support." That's about as ridiculous as the Gen Zers who think that self-management means: "Do whatever you want, whenever you want, however you want."

Both of these versions of "self-management" are fantasyland. They are the poles on opposite sides of the soft skills gap.

Gen Zers tend to see basic work habits as matters of personal choice or style and often do not see the concrete business reasons for the requirements or preferences of their managers. On the other hand, sometimes managers have strong preferences or requirements for which there is no true business reason. That is the prerogative of the employer. After all, you are paying your employees, not the other way around. But our advice to managers is to choose your battles carefully on these issues. Every requirement (or preference) you impose on Gen Zers is one you will have to pay for somehow in the bargain; it is one less element of flexibility you will have to offer in the employment value proposition, or at least it is one less bargaining chip you have.

For the most part, there are very good reasons for following established best practices when it comes to work habits:

- ◆ When employees are unwell, there are increased health care costs and absenteeism, as well as diminished performance and impact on morale.
- ◆ When employees do not attend to their grooming and attire and manners, they make a negative impression on those with whom they interact.
- ◆ When employees come in late, take long breaks, leave early, and miss deadlines, they add less value and they keep other people waiting.
- ◆ When employees don't take notes and use checklists and good systems of organization, they lose important information, lose track of what they are doing, and make it harder for others to coordinate with them.
- ◆ When employees don't pay attention to detail, they make more mistakes, causing diminished quality, and requiring rework.
- ◆ When employees cannot be counted on to follow through, projects are left unfinished, and others are distracted and inconvenienced by having to remind them.
- ◆ When employees do not take initiative, opportunities are missed, and problems go unsolved.

These are all very strong business reasons. But not all of them apply to all people in all jobs. Before you choose to impose a requirement or preference, at least interrogate yourself: What are the business reasons? And what is the cost to you in terms of your flexibility in sweetening your employment proposition to your employees?

What really matters, in your case, with your employees?

◆ When it comes to employee wellness:

◆ When it comes to employee self-presentation:

◆ When it comes to timeliness and employee work schedules:

◆ When it comes to meeting goals and deadlines:

◆ When it comes to using systems to stay organized:

◆ When it comes to employees paying attention to details:

◆ When it comes to follow-through:

◆ When it comes to taking initiative:

What really matters? My karate teacher, Frank Gorman, likes to say, "We are all creatures of our habits. Good habits? Bad habits? That is your choice."

What are you really prepared to require? What strong preferences are you prepared to impose? If they really matter, they are worth teaching.

TEACHING/LEARNING OBJECTIVE
Helping Gen Zers learn best practices and build better work habits when it comes to wellness, self-presentation, timeliness, organization, productivity, quality, follow-through, consistency, and initiative.

MAKE THEM AWARE/MAKE THEM CARE
Your script: "Here's why you should care about learning best practices and building better work habits: These basic work habits might seem like matters of personal style or preference. But in fact there

are strong business reasons for these requirements. How you present yourself and conduct yourself at work has a big impact on your performance and on all of those with whom you interact. Perhaps more to the point: It has a huge impact on your reputation at work.

"Not following good work habits with consistency makes you seem younger and less mature. It gives some managers second thoughts about trusting you with important work. If you want to be taken seriously in the workplace, your best bet is to learn best practices and develop good work habits. People will perceive you as being more professional. That will be very much to your benefit, both here and anywhere else you work.

"Here is the big challenge. What makes this hard is that habits are habits for a reason. Habits feel good. Habits feel right. Even if you can see the logic for a different set of behaviors that will have better results, it is very hard to break one habit and create a new one. Research shows that it takes several weeks of consistent practice of a new set of behaviors to form a new habit. It takes even longer for a new habit to become entrenched. But remember, human beings are not just creatures of habit. We are products of our habits. Will you be the product of good habits or bad habits? That is your choice."

Good Work Habits: Lesson Plan 1—Introduction

Consider the following "work habits" and what they mean to you:

◆ *Wellness:* Maintaining a healthy body, mind, and spirit/mood.
  • *Brainstorming questions:* What are the business reasons for employers to have strong guidelines or requirements for employees when it comes to wellness? What are the reasons why it is in your best interests as an employee to follow best practices when it comes to wellness? Are there good reasons to NOT follow best practices when it comes to wellness?

◆ *Self-presentation:* Controlling one's grooming, attire, and manners, given the social/cultural situation, so as to make a positive impression on others.
  • *Brainstorming questions:* What are the business reasons for employers to have strong guidelines or requirements for employees when it comes to self-presentation? What are the reasons why it is in your best interests as an employee to follow best practices when it comes to self-presentation? Are there good reasons to NOT follow best practices when it comes to self-presentation?

◆ *Timeliness:* Arriving early, staying late, and taking short breaks. Meeting or beating schedules and deadlines.
  • *Brainstorming questions:* What are the business reasons for employers to have strong guidelines or requirements for employees when it comes to timeliness? What are the reasons why it is in your best interests as an employee to follow best practices when it comes to timeliness? Are there good reasons to NOT follow best practices when it comes to timeliness?

◆ *Productivity:* Working at a fast pace without significant interruptions.
  • *Brainstorming questions:* What are the business reasons for employers to have strong guidelines or requirements for employees when it comes to productivity? What are the reasons why it is in your best interests as an employee to follow best practices when it comes to productivity? Are there good reasons to NOT follow best practices when it comes to productivity?

- *Organization:* Using proven systems for documentation and tracking such as note-taking, project plans, checklists, and filing.
  - *Brainstorming questions:* What are the business reasons for employers to have strong guidelines or requirements for employees when it comes to taking notes and using project plans, checklists, and filing systems? What are the reasons why it is in your best interests as an employee to follow best practices when it comes to taking notes and using project plans, checklists, and filing systems? Are there good reasons to NOT follow these best practices?
- *Attention to detail:* Following instructions, standard operating procedures, specifications, and staying focused and mindful in performing tasks and responsibilities.
  - *Brainstorming questions:* What are the business reasons for employers to have strong guidelines or requirements for employees when it comes to attention to detail? What are the reasons why it is in your best interests as an employee to follow best practices when it comes to attention to detail? Are there good reasons to NOT follow best practices when it comes to paying attention to detail?
- *Follow-through and consistency:* Fulfilling one's commitments and finishing what one starts.
  - *Brainstorming questions:* What are the business reasons for employers to have strong guidelines or requirements for employees when it comes to follow-through and consistency? What are the reasons why it is in your best interests as an employee to follow best practices when it comes to follow-through and consistency? Are there good reasons to NOT follow-through with consistency?
- *Initiative:* Self-starting. Taking productive action without explicit direction. Going above and beyond; the extra mile.
  - *Brainstorming questions:* What are the business reasons for employers to have strong guidelines or requirements for employees when it comes to initiative? What are the reasons why it is in your best interests as an employee to follow best practices when it comes to initiative? Are there good reasons to NOT take initiative?

Good Work Habits: Lesson Plan 2—Self-Assessment

Consider your own performance on the following "work habits":

- ◆ *Wellness:* Does this organization—your current employer—have specific guidelines and/or requirements for your wellness? Sleep requirements, body mass index, sobriety, certificates of fitness, continuing education, and so forth?
  - What are they? How are you doing personally when it comes to meeting these guidelines and requirements? Are you performing at 100 percent? If not, then what percentage would you give your performance? Where is the gap? What do you need to do to improve?
- ◆ *Self-presentation:* Does this organization—your current employer—have specific guidelines and/or requirements? Body mass index, height, hair length or style, dress code, uniform, etiquette, or others?
  - What are they? How are you doing personally when it comes to meeting these guidelines and requirements? Are you performing at 100 percent? If not, then what percentage would you give your performance? Where is the gap? What do you need to do to improve?
- ◆ *Timeliness:* Does this organization—your current employer—have specific guidelines and/or requirements? Shift schedules, arrival times, break times, departure times, and deadlines, etc.?
  - What are they? How are you doing personally when it comes to meeting these guidelines and requirements? Are you performing at 100 percent? If not, then what percentage would you give your performance? Where is the gap? What do you need to do to improve?
- ◆ *Productivity:* Does this organization—your current employer—have specific guidelines and/or requirements for productivity? Number of tasks completed per hour or per day, and so forth?
  - What are they? How are you doing personally when it comes to meeting these guidelines and requirements? Are you performing at 100 percent? If not, then what percentage would you give your performance? Where is the gap? What do you need to do to improve?

◆ *Organization:* Does this organization—your current employer—have specific guidelines and/or requirements for staying organized? Specific systems for documenting and tracking tasks, responsibilities, and projects; note-taking, checklists, project plans, filing, or other methods?
  • What are they? How are you doing personally when it comes to meeting these guidelines and requirements? Are you performing at 100 percent? If not, then what percentage would you give your performance? Where is the gap? What do you need to do to improve?
◆ *Attention to detail:* Does this organization—your current employer—have specific guidelines and/or requirements? Standard operating procedures, quality assurance, double-checking, triple-checking, or other methods?
  • What are they? How are you doing personally when it comes to meeting these guidelines and requirements? Are you performing at 100 percent? If not, then what percentage would you give your performance? Where is the gap? What do you need to do to improve?
◆ *Follow-through and consistency:* Does this organization—your current employer—have specific guidelines and/or requirements? Maximum response times, etc.?
  • What are they? How are you doing personally when it comes to meeting these guidelines and requirements? Are you performing at 100 percent? If not, then what percentage would you give your performance? Where is the gap? What do you need to do to improve?
◆ *Initiative:* Does this organization—your current employer—have specific guidelines and/or requirements?
  • Are you clear about what it looks like to go the extra mile in your current role? Do you know how far you are permitted to go, when going above and beyond? How far is too far—overstepping? What can you do better?

Good Work Habits: Lesson Plan 3—Self-Improvement Planning

Make a plan for improving your "work habits":

- *Wellness:* What are the requirements? What is your personal goal for improvement in the near future? What resources and support are available? What is your plan? What is your first step? When?

- *Self-presentation:* What are the requirements? What is your personal goal for improvement in the near future? What resources and support are available? What is your plan? What is your first step? When?

- *Timeliness:* What are the requirements? What is your personal goal for improvement in the near future? What resources and support are available? What is your plan? What is your first step? When?

- *Productivity:* What are the requirements? What is your personal goal for improvement in the near future? What resources and support are available? What is your plan? What is your first step? When?

- *Organization:* What are the requirements? What is your personal goal for improvement in the near future? What resources and support are available? What is your plan? What is your first step? When?

- *Attention to detail:* What are the requirements? What is your personal goal for improvement in the near future? What resources and support are available? What is your plan? What is your first step? When?

- *Follow-through and consistency:* What are the requirements? What is your personal goal for improvement in the near future? What resources and support are available? What is your plan? What is your first step? When?

- *Initiative:* What are the requirements? What is your personal goal for improvement in the near future? What resources and support are available? What is your plan? What is your first step? When?

Good Work Habits: Lesson Plan 4—Wellness

Consider Wellness: Maintaining a healthy body, mind, and spirit/mood.

- ◆ Are you taking good care of your mind? What are the main sources of input for your mind right now? How can you expose your mind to a greater variety of input?
- ◆ Are you taking good care of your body? When do you sleep? What do you eat and drink? How do you exercise? What bad habits do you need to break?
- ◆ Are you taking good care of your mood/spirit? How is your mood right now? How is your mood usually? What sources of strength—teachers, friends, family, music, prayer, meditation, exercise, games, hobbies, art, etc.—can you tap more often that will lift your spirit/mood?
- ◆ What are your goals?
  - • For taking good care of your mind:

  - • For taking good care of your body:

  - • For taking good care of your spirit/mood/:

- ◆ What resources and support might be available?
- ◆ What is your plan?
- ◆ What is your first step? When?

Good Work Habits: Lesson Plan 5—Planning a Wellness Initiative

There are many different approaches to employer-sponsored employee wellness programs, including a wide range of potential services and products. Here are some of the most common approaches (and some very uncommon) for you to consider:

- Education on wellness best practices, provided internally or externally. This can be achieved through newsletters, flyers, videos, websites, apps, or through classes and discussion groups. These efforts typically focus on the most significant controllable variables—diet, exercise, sleep, substance use (especially tobacco), and dealing with common stressors
- Exercise programs, either offered on site or reimbursement for those offered externally
- Healthful eating programs, including nutritional information and healthful food choices in cafeterias and kitchens at work
- Weight-loss programs, ranging from on-site support groups to employee competitions
- Smoking cessation programs
- Substance-abuse cessation programs
- Stress reduction and management programs
- Anti-bullying programs
- Online (or telephone) health advisors/coaches
- On-site health care services, ranging from periodic health risk screenings and flu shots and the like to full-scale on-site health care clinics, complete with doctors, nurses, dentists, and more
- Walking meetings and/or "stretching" meetings
- Ergonomic workspace and furniture
- Napping rooms that can double as meditation rooms
- Game rooms offering games ranging from old-fashioned Ping-Pong to newfangled videogames
- Massage and other spa-like services

Step One   Inventory your current resources. Find out what your organization currently offers or currently supports and determine whether there might be resources easily obtained to offer or support additional programs.

Of course, some of what your organization supports will be obvious. You probably already know whether there is a company cafeteria with a "healthy food" option every day or an on-site gym or a lunchtime walking group or an after work yoga class.

But there may be policies (and accompanying resources) that are less obvious. For example, some organizations support wellness by offering discounts on health insurance premiums to those who participate in wellness programs or who meet certain benchmarks on key risk variables such as body mass, blood pressure, smoking, substance use, etc.. Meanwhile, some employers impose penalties on employees who do not participate or who fail to meet certain benchmarks.

Do some research internally using the list above (and anything else you can think of) to see what your organization already offers or supports or might be willing to support. Ask your boss. Ask HR. Look online. Ask around.

Step Two   Choose a point of focus for your wellness initiative. You could always make a decree as the manager and choose a point of focus for a wellness program for your team and see whether they go along with it:

- From now on, one-on-one meetings will be walking meetings.
- Lunchtime or after work exercise group—running or yoga or whatever.
- Massage therapist will be coming around once a week.
- Weight loss competition: Who can lose the most weight?

But you will almost surely gain much greater interest and more enthusiastic participation if they participate in choosing the focus. Bring the team together and have a group discussion. Sometimes there will be a strong consensus to focus on one thing or another. In a larger team, there may be small groups that coalesce around one focus or another.

Step Three   Remember that most of the meaningful efforts employees can make to improve their own wellness will have to be done on their own time at their own initiative.

Encourage employees to share their wellness goals up-front and share their progress along the way: One thing you can do is provide recognition, credit, or possibly rewards for those who meet specific wellness goals. (My advice is to talk to your boss or someone in HR and see what resources might be available and whether doing so would be in keeping with your organization's policies.)

Good Work Habits: Lesson Plan 6—Self-Presentation

Complete the following brainstorming exercise:

◆ *Self-presentation:* Controlling one's grooming, attire, and manners, given the social/cultural situation, so as to make a positive impression on others.
  • How would you describe your current approach to self-presentation?
  • Grooming:

  • Attire:

  • Manners:

◆ In this organization are their formal requirements or guidelines for self-presentation?
  • Grooming: Hair, cleanliness, etc.?
  • Attire: Is there a uniform?
  • Manners: "Yes, sir. Yes, ma'am," etc.?

◆ What about informally: In this organization are there informal guidelines that most people follow?
  • Grooming: Hair, cleanliness, etc.?
  • Attire: Is there a uniform?
  • Manners: "Yes, sir. Yes, ma'am," etc.?
◆ What is the message being sent by the guidelines in this organization, whether formal or informal?
◆ What is the message that you want to send when it comes to your self-presentation?
◆ Where do you fit in relation to the informal or formal guidelines in this organization? What message does that send?
  • Grooming: Hair, cleanliness, etc.?
  • Attire: Is there a uniform?
  • Manners: "Yes, sir. Yes, ma'am," etc.?
Is there anything you should change about yourself?

Good Work Habits: Lesson Plan 7—Using a Time Log to Start Living by a Schedule

Learning to maintain an old-fashioned time log is a great way to begin to understand how you actually use your time inside and outside of work. The tool is very simple, but the insights can be profound when you see how you actually use that precious limited resource—your time.

Step One   Using the time-log tool here, think back over the last 24 hours and try to reconstruct exactly how you used your time—hour by hour. Start with right now and work backward 24 hours or so, noting as best you can, hour by hour, what you were doing:

Today	Yesterday
12:01 am	
1	
2	
3	
4	
5	
6	
7	
8	
9	
10	
11	
1	
2	
3	
4	
5	
6	
7	
8	
9	
10	
11	
11:59 pm	

Step Two   Now look back over the past 24-hour time log you just completed. Is this a typical 24-hour period? If not, go back and make notes about where your typical day might differ from the last 24-hours.

Step Three   Now make a list of your top priorities in life and at work.

Step Four   Compare your list of top priorities with your time log for a typical 24-hour period. How does your time spending line up with your top priorities?

Step Five   Look at your own schedule.

STOP: Do you keep a schedule? Do you live by a schedule? If you do not already keep a schedule, take out your hand-held device. You almost surely already have multiple scheduling apps, complete with automated reminders, from which you can choose. Choose one and make a note to familiarize yourself with it.

Write out your schedule for the coming 24 hours, hour by hour.

Today	Tomorrow
12:01 am	
1	
2	
3	
4	
5	
6	
7	
8	
9	
10	
11	
1	
2	
3	
4	
5	

Today	Tomorrow
6	
7	
8	
9	
10	
11	
11:59 pm	

Now take a look and ask yourself: How does that schedule for the next 24 hours line up with my top priorities? Are there any changes you need to make?

Step Six   Now consider your schedule for the coming week.

STOP: If you are just familiarizing yourself with a scheduling app, this is the time to schedule some key appointments for the coming week:

- ◆ What time do you arrive for work each day? Plug in your arrival time for work each day.
- ◆ How much time do you need to get to work? Plug in a reminder to depart for work on time each day.
- ◆ How much time do you need to get ready for work before you depart? Plug in an alarm to start getting ready.

Now fill in key appointments for the coming week.

Now take a look at your schedule for the coming week and ask yourself: How does my schedule line up with my top priorities? Are there any changes I need to make?

Step Seven   HOMEWORK: Keep a real-time time log for the next week. Do it hour-by-hour or in fifteen-minute increments. Every time you switch activities, take note. Do it for a whole week.

Step Eight   AFTER COMPLETING HOMEWORK: Evaluate your full-week real-time time log:

- Examine your time log to identify your biggest time-wasters. What are your lowest priority activities that are taking up your time? How can you eliminate them?
- Examine your time log to identify your biggest interruptions. What can you do to better manage those interruptions?
- Examine your time log to identify any unexpected emergencies or urgent matters that required your attention. What can you do to better anticipate and prevent those emergencies/urgencies going forward?
- Examine your time log to identify opportunities to increase your efficiency. What can you streamline? What shortcuts can you take? What detours can you avoid?

Now make your schedule for the coming week, taking into account what you've learned from keeping the time log.

Step Nine   Repeat Steps Seven and Eight for as many weeks in a row as possible.

Good Work Habits: Lesson Plan 8—How to Make a Basic Project Plan

Step One   Choose your most important project on which to focus.

- ◆ What is the big goal? What is the deadline? What are the specifications?

Step Two   Working backward from the deadline, break that big goal into intermediate goals with intermediate deadlines:

Intermediate Goals	Intermediate Deadlines

Step Three   Working backward from each intermediate goal and deadline, break each intermediate goal and deadline into a timetable of concrete action steps.

Intermediate Goals	Intermediate Deadlines	Action Steps/Timetable
Intermediate goal	Intermediate deadline	
		1
		2
		3
		4
		5
Intermediate goal	Intermediate deadline	
		1
		2
		3
		4
		5

Intermediate Goals	Intermediate Deadlines	Action Steps/Timetable
Intermediate goal	Intermediate deadline	
		1
		2
		3
		4
		5

Step Four   Now make a step-by-step plan going forward, with a time budget for each action step, from day one until the final deadline. Every day consult your step-by-step plan, and make a list of action steps, noting the time budget you have allowed and any guidelines and specifications. That's how to bring a plan alive and put it into action: Use it every day to make your to-do list.

Step Five   Make sure to track your progress and make sure you are meeting your timetables for each concrete action step along the way to each intermediate deadline. Track your progress to make sure you are meeting each intermediate deadline. If you are off track, revisit the plan, then revise and adjust your timetables . . . or speed up!

Good Work Habits: Lesson Plan 9—Taking Notes and Making Checklists

Step One   Make a list of your recurring tasks or responsibilities.

Step Two   Take it one task/responsibility at a time. Start with your number one task/responsibility.
Brainstorm:

- What information do you need to return to regularly? How do you keep track of it? What can you do to take better notes?
- What information will you want to pass on to someone else? How do you keep track of it? What can you do to take better notes?
- What information will you need to return to at a specific time in the future? How do you keep track of it? What can you do to take better notes?

Now go through the rest of your tasks/responsibilities and answer the questions above for each one.

Step Three   Brainstorm: What is your current system for taking notes and keeping track of information? How can you improve on your current system?

Step Four   Brainstorm: What information tools do you currently have available to you in order to help you keep track of that information? Do you currently use checklists to guide you? On which tasks/responsibilities would checklists be helpful tools to guide you?

Step Five   Make checklists to guide you on any recurring task or responsibility. Take it one task/responsibility at a time. All checklists really are is a list of very detailed step-by-step instructions:

- First, write out step-by-step instructions for the task, from memory: Break each task into its component steps; and break each step into a series of concrete actions.

- Second, perform the task, very slowly, keeping one eye on the step-by-step instructions you prepared. As you perform the task, make corrections and additions to your instructions.
- Third, perform the task again, very slowly, and make further corrections and additions. Include as many details on each step—and in between each step—as you can think of. Make a checklist for each item within the checklist. Seriously: Take each step and break it down into smaller pieces so there is a mini-checklist for each item.
- Fourth, write a new draft, that is, step-by-step instructions in the form of a checklist.
- Fifth, ask someone else to try using your checklist to guide him or her and see whether it works. Ask for suggestions for further corrections and additions.
- Sixth, going forward, use this checklist to guide you in completing your task and also for making notes along the way. Remember, the key is actually using the checklists. You have to "check" as you complete each item on the checklist. Make notes in the margins of the checklists as you use them.

Good Work Habits: Lesson Plan 10—Doing a Time/Motion Study on Yourself

Step One   Make a list of your recurring tasks or responsibilities. Take it one task/responsibility at a time. Start with your number one task/responsibility.

Step Two   For this task, if you have a checklist, use the checklist to help you do your time/motion study. You'll need to actually perform the task to do this time/motion study properly:

- One task at a time, do the task multiple times.
- If you don't already have a checklist, you'll have to break each task into its component steps and break each step into a series of concrete actions.
- As you perform the task, time the whole task; time each step within each task; time each concrete action within each step.
- How long does each task take? Each step within each task? Each concrete action within each step? How long should they take? Create a time budget for every concrete action for every step and for every task.

That's a time/motion study.

Step Three   Take it to the next level by using your time/motion budgets to help you keep score for yourself going forward.

- If you are behind schedule: Do a micro-gap analysis. Identify the micro-gaps between the time budget you made and your actual time step-by-step, concrete action by concrete action. In these micro-gaps lie the potential opportunities to speed up.
- If you want to speed up: Choose one concrete action at a time to "accelerate" and take it slowly. Close the micro-gaps one by one. By going one concrete action at time, you will minimize the chances of increased mistakes in the effort to "speed up."
- Are you sure you are doing each concrete step correctly?
- Are you doing any unnecessary actions or steps that might slow you down?
- Are you encountering any recurring obstacles that can be removed?

Good Work Habits: Lesson Plan 11—Spotlight on Follow-Through

Step One   Brainstorm. What does it mean to you to "follow through" on your commitments at work? Why is follow-through important?

Step Two   Make a list of all of your current tasks, responsibilities and projects. For each one, make note of the following: What is your next deliverable and when is it due? What was the last time you took action on it? What is the next step you need to take to move that task/responsibility/or project forward?

Tasks/Projects	Next Deliverable	Last Action Taken	Next Step

Step Three   What can you do to close out work that should not still be open?

Good Work Habits: Lesson Plan 12—Going the Extra Mile

Step One   Brainstorm. What does it mean to you to "take initiative" at work? What does it mean to "go the extra mile"? What does it mean to go "above and beyond"?

Step Two   Make a list of all of your current tasks, responsibilities, and projects. What are all the aspects of doing your job very well, very fast, all day long?

Step Three   Now, next to each task, responsibility, and project, take note: What would it look like for you to go the extra mile on that task, responsibility, or project? After you do your job very well, very fast, all day long—in those extra moments—what are some extra ways you can add value?

Make an "extra mile" list for yourself, a list of all the extra ways you can go above and beyond on every task, responsibility, or project.

Step Four   HOMEWORK. Every single item on your extra mile list is a concrete opportunity to excel in your current role. How often do you complete items on your extra mile list? Keep score for yourself going forward.

How to Teach People Skills

People skills: Attentive listening, observing, and reading; perceiving and empathizing; effective and appropriate use of words, tone, expressions, and gestures—verbal, written, and otherwise—one-on-one and in groups, in person and remotely.

THE GAP

> *Manager:* "They want constant feedback, yet most of them won't even pick up the phone or make an effort to talk in person, even when we are in the same place at the same time and, when they do, it makes you kind of wish they hadn't. . . . They want to be invited to the important meetings, but then show up late or play with their phones during the meeting. Even email is passé to them so they send emails that look like texts."
>
> *Gen Zer:* "Seriously?! Why waste so much time and so many words? Anyway, texting gives me a little space. Meeting in person or on the phone makes me feel kind of uncomfortable, like I'm on the spot all of a sudden."

THE BRIDGE: WHAT YOU, THE MANAGER, NEED TO REMEMBER

Are Gen Zers' relatively weak people skills simply the result of becoming so accustomed to communicating with their devices that they are losing the ability to communicate well in person and on the phone?

That's surely a big part of the story. Communication practices are habits, and most Gen Zers are in the habit of remote informal staccato and relatively low-stakes interpersonal communication because of their constant use of hand-held devices and the mores of social media and instant messaging.

The crux of people skills is "other orientation," paying close attention to the signals of those with whom one is interacting, without getting distracted, and then responding to those signals effectively and appropriately. But Gen Zers are very self-focused. Plus, they are often distracted. And they are so unaccustomed to engaging in person and on the telephone that their powers of perception are often not well developed. No wonder they are not very good at reading people, especially in person and on the phone.

Think of it this way: Have you ever had a big misunderstanding (or fight) with someone via text messaging? Often that happens because words alone, especially informal staccato messages, are very easy to misunderstand. That's because tone, expressions, and gestures are a very big part of how human beings communicate. So much meaning is lost or misconstrued in texts. Now throw in the social media dimension in which communication is an interactive performance among peers (or not even peers, but the virtual personas of peers). This is the information environment in which Gen Zers honed their interpersonal communication practices. Even their in-person interactions—especially with their peers—are almost always underwritten and mediated by their social media network relationships. No wonder they so often say the wrong things at the wrong times.

Building relationships in the relatively formal high-stakes real world of the workplace is a brand new challenge for Gen Zers. School is probably their closest analogue. But in school, Gen Zers have been largely spoon-fed the structure and substance of their important formal communication. In the workplace, they are less likely to be spoon-fed.

Yes, there is structure in most workplaces. Nonetheless, a shocking amount of the important communication in most workplaces is largely ad hoc, hit and miss. There is a lot of "touching base" and "call me if you need me" and mediocre meetings and long multi-recipient email chains, but there is usually way too little regular, structured communication. This is one reason why Gen Zers don't treat interpersonal communication in the workplace with greater formality. No wonder Gen Zers don't realize that the burden is on them to ensure their interpersonal communication at work is more structured and substantive. Like any other habits, communication habits can be changed, but it is not easy.

If you are the leader, then you should take on more of the burden yourself of making sure that your communication with your Gen Zers (and all of your employees, for that matter) is high structure and high substance. Engage every single Gen Zer in a regular structured one-on-one dialogue, scheduling one-on-ones at least once a week. The one-on-ones with you will give them the chance to practice interacting in a more professional manner—at least with you. As you fine-tune your ongoing dialogue with each Gen Zer, he or she will become accustomed to your one-on-ones. Over time, you will help them learn to prepare better and better agendas for your one-on-ones; increasingly organized, clear, and focused.

TEACHING/LEARNING OBJECTIVE

Helping Gen Zers learn best practices and build better habits when it comes to interpersonal communication—people skills.

MAKE THEM AWARE/MAKE THEM CARE

Your script: "Here's why you should care about improving your people skills: Even though it seems like your interactions with other people are a matter of personal style, in fact, there are proven best practices for workplace communication. When people do not follow communication best practices, things are much more likely to go wrong. Poor communication is the number one cause of unnecessary problems—great and small—in the workplace.

"Poor communication also leads to suboptimal workplace relationships, including conflicts between and among employees.

"No matter where you work or what you do, good people skills will help you get ahead faster. Poor people skills will always hold you back. Some people are known as being really great to work with, while others are known for being difficult. In either case, that's almost always a commentary on the person's communication practices. You want to be known as someone who is great to work with.

"That means you need to learn best practices and build new habits to . . .

- ◆ Learn how to tune in to other people and read them more effectively;
- ◆ Take on the burden of putting more structure and substance into your communication with key people; and
- ◆ Learn best practices for expressing yourself more effectively—one-on-one and in groups, in person and remotely.

"If you learn those best practices and develop better habits, you will avoid many more unnecessary problems, you will build much better workplace relationships, and you will become one of those people with a reputation for being really great to work with."

People Skills: Lesson Plan 1—Interpersonal Communication

Consider the following "interpersonal communication" best practices and what they mean to you. For each one, use these questions for brainstorming: What are the business reasons for this best practice? What are the reasons why it is in your best interests as an employee to follow this best practice? Are there good reasons to NOT follow this best practice?

- Listen twice as much as you talk.
- Never interrupt or let your mind wander when others are speaking.
- Empathize: Always try to imagine yourself in the other person's position.
- Exhibit respect, kindness, courtesy, and good manners.
- Prepare in advance before meetings or one-on-one conversations so you are brief, direct, and clear.
- Never speak of a problem unless you have thought of at least one potential solution.
- Take personal responsibility for everything you say and do.
- Don't make excuses when you make a mistake.
- Don't blame or complain.
- Don't take yourself too seriously.
- Always take your commitments and responsibilities seriously.
- Always give people credit for their achievements, no matter how small.

People Skills: Lesson Plan 2—Self-Assessing Interpersonal Communication

Consider your own personal track record when it comes to the following "interpersonal communication" best practices. For each one: Give yourself a grade (+A–, +B–, +C–, +D–, F) for your track record so far and consider what you can do to improve on that best practice.

- Listen twice as much as you talk.
- Never interrupt or let your mind wander when others are speaking.
- Empathize: Always try to imagine yourself in the other person's position.
- Exhibit respect, kindness, courtesy, and good manners.
- Prepare in advance before meetings or one-on-one conversations so you are brief, direct, and clear.
- Never speak of a problem unless you have thought of at least one potential solution.
- Take personal responsibility for everything you say and do.
- Don't make excuses when you make a mistake.
- Don't blame or complain.
- Don't take yourself too seriously.
- Always take your commitments and responsibilities seriously.
- Always give people credit for their achievements, no matter how small.

People Skills: Lesson Plan 3—Learning to Use the "People List"

Step One Make a list of all the key people you interact with at work on a regular basis and put them into the following categories:

- ◆ Leaders, managers, and supervisors to whom you report directly or indirectly
- ◆ Co-workers on your team
- ◆ Co-workers outside your team
- ◆ Anyone who directly reports to you as their manager
- ◆ Outside partners or vendors

Step Two Now take them one person at a time. For each person on your list, answer the following questions:

Who?

- ◆ Who is this person at work? What role does this person play in relation to you and your job? Is this person highly regarded by others, as far as you know? Do you hold this person in high regard?

Why?

- ◆ What is your primary reason for interacting with this person at work?
- ◆ What are the circumstances that cause you to interact with this person? What are the conditions? What are you trying to accomplish in your interactions with this person? What are your goals for your interactions with this person?

What?

- ◆ What is the substance of the communication you need to have with this person?
- ◆ What do you need to learn from this communication? What does the other person need from you? What information exchange do you need to accomplish? What are the right words?

How?

◆ How do you usually interact with this person? Do you ask questions? Or do you give instructions? Do you spell things out in detail? Or are you specific or vague? Are you direct or indirect?

◆ How do you think this person would prefer you interact?

Where?

◆ If you meet in person, then where do you meet usually? If you do not meet in person, then where do the conversations take place: By telephone? Email? Text? Or otherwise? One-on-one? In meetings?

◆ Where do you think this person would prefer to interact?

When?

◆ When do you usually interact with this person? What days and times typically? And how often?

◆ When do you think this person would prefer to interact with you?

This is a great tool to help you tune in better to any person with whom you need to interact on a regular basis. You can use this tool any time you want to try to better understand where a person is coming from and how to be more effective in your communication practices with this person.

Step Three Take this exercise to the next level by turning these six questions into a powerful tool for staying tuned in to other people at work and maintaining better interpersonal communication.

Arrange the six questions (just the shorthand) along the top of a page in a horizontal axis, either on paper or in a simple spreadsheet. In the "Who" column, write the names of all the key people with whom you interact. Then make some notes in answer to the question: "Who is this person in relation to you at work?" Then, for each person, answer the other five questions and make some notes in each column alongside that person's name in the same horizontal row. Answer all the questions for everybody on your list. That's how you make a "people list."

Who	Why	What	How	Where	When

Step Four After you've made your first people list, it shouldn't be your last.

HOMEWORK. Try making a people list at least once a week. Do it at the beginning of each week. Set up the columns. Then make a list of the key people with whom you need to interact that week: leaders, co-workers, direct reports, and anyone else. Go through and make some notes in answer to each of the six questions for each person. That's a great way to set yourself up for success in your interpersonal communication that week!

Step Five Take this exercise even further by using a slightly different version of this tool to interview the key people with whom you interact and asking them directly how they would like you to structure your interpersonal communication with them going forward.

Who?

♦ How would you describe the role you play here? From your perspective, where do I fit in relation to you?

Why?

♦ From your perspective, what is the primary reason we interact? What do you need to accomplish when interacting with me? What should my goals be when I am interacting with you?

What?

♦ What is the substance of the communication we need to have? What should I be trying to learn from this communication? What do you need to learn from me? What information do you need from me? What are the right words for me to say to you?

How?

♦ How would you prefer we interact? Would you prefer that I ask questions or just answer questions? Do you want to give me instructions or do you need instructions from me? Do you need things in detail or just the big picture?

Where?

◆ Does meeting in person work better for you? If so, where would you prefer to meet? If meeting in person is not an option, then where do you prefer the conversations take place: By telephone? Email? Text? Or otherwise? One-on-one? In meetings?

When?

◆ What days and times work best for you? How often do you think we need to meet?

Consider taking the time to interview all the key people with whom you interact. Use the interviews as a learning process and as an opportunity to plan together with each person for how you will communicate going forward.

People Skills: Lesson Plan 4—Putting More Structure into Your Communication

Step One   High structure means regularly scheduled and conducted according to a clear well organized agenda with lots of give and take.

Brainstorming questions: How many of your important conversations at work are high structure by this definition? Which ones are high structure? Which ones are low structure? Why?

Step Two   What can you do to put more structure into more of your important conversations?

- ◆ Can you schedule them? Which ones? When?
- ◆ Can you create a clear, well-organized agenda? For which ones?
- ◆ What can you do to put more give and take into your conversations? Are you usually giving or taking? Can you adjust the balance?

Step Three   Look at your schedule. Or consider your typical day or week. How much time can you set aside each day for regular structured communication? Can you block out time every day? Every other day? Twice a week? How many scheduled one-on-one conversations can you fit into that time?

Step Four   Make a list of the key people with whom you need to interact: your managers, co-workers inside and outside your team, your direct reports, and anyone else. Start with the most important conversations and schedule as many one-on-one conversations as you can squeeze in.

Step Five   Consider the following best practices.

- ◆ Is it possible to choose a regular time and stick with it as long as you can? If you have to make a change, try to set a new regular time and try to stick with the new time as long as you can.

- ◆ Is it possible to have in-person meetings? If you have to meet remotely, don't let the phone call slip. Be sure to support these telephone conversations with clear point-by-point emails before and after your calls. Follow-up emails are key, especially following telephone one-on-ones.
- ◆ Is it possible to meet in the same place? Choose a good venue, whether it is your office, a conference room, or the stairwell. You want these meetings to become familiar and comfortable. The routine of meeting in the same place every time is an important part of the structure these one-on-one meetings provide.

People Skills: Lesson Plan 5—Putting More Substance into Your Communication

Step One High substance means rich in relevant information.

Brainstorming questions: How many of your important conversations at work are high substance by this definition? Which ones are high substance? Which ones are low substance? Why? What's the difference?

Step Two Look at your schedule or consider your typical day or week.

- ◆ Make a list of the key people with whom you need to interact: Your managers, co-workers inside and outside your team, your direct reports, and anyone else.
- ◆ Make a list of conversations you anticipate having in the next week.

Step Three Review the list above of conversations you anticipate having and schedule as many of these conversations as possible.

Step Four Choose one of the anticipated conversations to zero in on. Ask yourself what you can do to better prepare for the conversation:

- ◆ What can you do to prepare in advance?
- ◆ Do you have a clear agenda for the meeting?
- ◆ What information do you need to deliver, in what form?
  - • Is there a document you can prepare in advance to make it more clear?
  - • What key points will you want to address verbally? Make a list of those key points.
- ◆ What information do you need to capture and in what form?
  - • Is there an information-capture tool you can prepare in advance to make it easier?
  - • What key questions will you want to ask? Make a list of key questions.

◆ Are there some parts of the conversation that might be difficult? If so, consider writing a script and even rehearsing it before the conversation. (You don't have to stick exactly to the script, but it might help you if you are nervous or thrown off during the actual conversation.)

◆ Be prepared to wrap up each conversation with the following questions:

- Exactly what is my next deliverable on this? To whom? By what deadline?
- What guidelines and specifications should I follow?
- Do you want me to prepare a short step-by-step plan first and run it by you?
- When should we talk next? Let's schedule our next conversation now: When? Where? What will be our agenda?

Step Five   HOMEWORK. Use this tool going forward to prepare in advance for conversations. Modify it any way you like to make it more useful.

People Skills: Lesson Plan 6—Preparing for Meetings

Step One   Consider the following best practices for preparing for meetings. For each one. Give yourself a grade (+A–, +B–, +C–, +D–, F) for your track record so far.

- ◆ Before attending any meeting or presentation, make sure you know what the meeting is about and whether your attendance is required or requested.
- ◆ Identify what your role in the meeting is. What information are you responsible for communicating or gathering?

Prepare in advance:

- ◆ Is there any material you should review or read before the meeting? Are there any conversations you need to have before the meeting?
- ◆ If you are making a presentation, prepare even more. Ask yourself exactly what value you have to offer the group.
- ◆ If you are not a primary actor in the meeting, often the best thing you can do is say as little as possible and practice good meeting manners: Do not "multi-task," make unnecessary noise or activity, and do stay focused on the business at hand.
- ◆ If you are tempted to speak up, ask yourself: Is this a point that everyone needs to hear, right here and now? If you have a question, could it be asked at a later time, off-line?
- ◆ If you don't have a clear role in the meeting and yet find yourself there anyway, try not to say a single word that will unnecessarily lengthen it.

Step Two   Go back through the same list of best practices. Take them one by one. For each one, brainstorm using these questions: What are the business reasons for this best practice? What are the reasons why it is in your best interests as an employee to follow this best practice? Are there good reasons to NOT follow this best practice? What can you do to improve?

People Skills: Lesson Plan 7—Email Best Practices

Step One   Consider the following best practices for email communication. For each one. Give yourself a grade (+A–, +B–, +C–, +D–, F) for your track record so far.

- Send fewer and better messages.
- Before sending a message, always ask yourself whether this is really something that should be communicated in person at a scheduled one-on-one or a scheduled meeting.
- Stop sending first drafts! Send first drafts to yourself.
- If you are "messaging" so you don't forget, then send the reminder to yourself!
- Only cc people who need to be cc'd.
- Use red flags and other indicators sparingly and with true purpose.
- Make subject lines smart; context is everything.
- Change subject lines on later emails if the subject changes.
- Make messages brief, simple, and orderly.
- Create a simple folder system for filing incoming and outgoing electronic communication based on how YOU will use them later.
- Establish time blocks daily when you will review and respond to electronic communication and let people know when to expect your responses

Step Two   Go back through the same list of best practices. Take them one by one. For each one, brainstorm using these questions: What are the business reasons for this best practice? What are the reasons why it is in your best interests as an employee to follow this best practice? Are there good reasons to NOT follow this best practice? What can you do to improve?

People Skills: Lesson Plan 8—Communicating Remotely

Step One   Consider the following best practices for remote communication. For each one. Give yourself a grade (+A–, +B–, +C–, +D–, F) for your track record so far.

+ Keep each other informed about when you'll both be at a central location, such as the organization's headquarters, so you can schedule in-person one-on-one time.
+ Schedule occasional in-person meetings when it is convenient for you to visit your remotely located interlocutor or when it is convenient for Remote to visit you in your location.
+ If you have even simple video phone capability, consider meeting sometimes via video phone.
+ In the absence of in-person meetings and two-way web-cams, make good use of regular telephone and electronic communication.
+ Schedule regular one-on-one telephone calls with your remotely located interlocutor and never miss the calls.
+ Prepare in advance of your one-on-ones. Prepare in advance a written recap of highlights and key issues since your last one-on-one call, as well as open questions to discuss during the one-on-one.
+ Immediately following each call, send an email recapping what you both agreed on in your conversation: the actions you are each expected to take, the steps you will follow, and the timeline; as well as the date and time of your next scheduled phone call; and then, of course, prepare in advance and send any documents for review prior to the next meeting.

Step Two   Go back through the same list of best practices. Take them one by one. For each one, brainstorm using these questions: What are the business reasons for this best practice? What are the reasons why it is in your best interests as an employee to follow this best practice? Are there good reasons to NOT follow this best practice? What can you do to improve?

Chapter 5

How to Teach the Missing Basics of Critical Thinking to Today's Young Talent

Critical Thinking: The Missing Basics

Proactive learning: Keeping an open mind, suspending judgment, questioning assumptions, and seeking out information, technique and perspective; and studying, practicing, and contemplating in order to build one's stored knowledge base, skill-set, and wisdom.

Problem solving: Mastering established best-practices—proven repeatable solutions for dealing with regularly recurring decisions—so as to avoid reinventing the wheel. Using repeatable solutions to improvise when addressing problems that are new but similar.

Decision making: Identifying and considering multiple options, assessing the pros and cons of each, and choosing the course of action closest to the desired outcome.

How to Teach Proactive Learning

Proactive learning: Keeping an open mind, suspending judgment, questioning assumptions, and seeking out information, technique, and perspective, and studying, practicing, and contemplating in order to build one's stored knowledge base, skill-set, and wisdom.

THE GAP

> *Manager:* "It's like they think they know everything because they can always find the right answer on their phones, but they don't realize they don't have the experience to really understand the answers they can find so easily."
>
> *Gen Zer:* "I don't even need to know anything really. There is no such thing as a learning curve anymore."

THE BRIDGE: WHAT YOU, THE MANAGER, NEED TO REMEMBER

Before any individual can possibly succeed at "critical thinking," that person has to know some things. That way he or she will have something—anything really—about which to think critically. Step One: Know something! Or know how to do something! Or have an appreciation for multiple competing perspectives about something—anything really.

It is almost a hackneyed truth about today's world that we all have endless amounts of information at our fingertips available instantly all the time. Indeed, we have multiple competing answers to any question on any subject—more answers than a whole platoon could possibly master in a lifetime on any subject. It is nearly as hackneyed to say that today's new young workforce has never known it any other way. The not quite as obvious punch line is this: There has been a radical change in the prevailing mindset about how much information a person needs to keep inside the head versus accessible through the fingertips. Nobody should be so short-sighted or so old-fashioned as to write off the power of being able to find multiple competing answers to any question about any subject any time instantly. Yet this phenomenon is also at the root of the "critical thinking" skills gap.

Critical thinking is very difficult. It requires strong thinking muscles. Like any muscles, thinking muscles don't get strong overnight. If you're not in shape, you start by taking walks, not distance runs. If you've never lifted weights, you have to start off with lighter weights and work yourself up to the heavier lifting.

Critical thinking is also a very sophisticated skill-set. It requires mental flexibility and agility. But if you try to stretch too much too fast without good form and good structural support, you are liable to pull a muscle. When it comes to critical thinking, stupid decisions are the equivalent of pulled muscles.

What is the best way to "build strong thinking muscles"? Exercise them regularly. That means studying information, practicing technique, and contemplating multiple competing perspectives.

What is the necessary "structural support"? Stored knowledge, skill, and wisdom.

Good news:

- Stored knowledge is the result of studying good information.
- Stored skills are the result of practicing good technique.
- Stored wisdom is the result of contemplating multiple competing good perspectives.

What is "good form"? Keeping an open mind. That means suspending judgment, questioning assumptions, and continually seeking out the best new information, technique, and perspective.

That's why proactive learning is the first of the missing basics of critical thinking.

TEACHING/LEARNING OBJECTIVE

Help them develop the habits of keeping an open mind by honing the skills of suspending judgment, questioning assumptions, and seeking out information, technique, and perspective and helping them develop greater stored knowledge, skills, and wisdom by honing the skills of studying, practicing, and contemplating.

MAKE THEM AWARE/MAKE THEM CARE

Your script: "Here's why you should care about proactive learning. Of course, the more you learn, the more you will know. But there is more to it than that. All the leading research shows that the very act of learning also strengthens your mind. If you are not actively learning, then your mind is getting weaker—just like any muscle. No matter how smart you are, if you are not actively learning, then you are actually becoming a little dumber every day. You probably won't notice. However, all the leading research says this is the case.

"Even if you don't learn anything, the very act of trying to learn is great exercise for your brain. Your mind needs regular exercise to stay in shape and get stronger.

"Critical thinking skills are incredibly valuable—among the most in-demand skills in nearly every sector of the labor market. The reason they are so valuable and in demand is because they are considered to be in relatively short supply. That's because critical thinking is a whole lot harder than it looks. Critical thinkers do not leap to conclusions; they take the time to consider various possibilities and do not become too attached to one point of view. They do not latch on to one solution; they know that most solutions are temporary and improve over time with new data. They are in the habit of trying to differentiate between reliable and unreliable sources. They carefully weigh the strengths of conflicting views and apply logical reasoning. Critical thinkers are, at once, open to the views of others and supremely independent in their own judgments.

"Think of the very smartest person you know. You can take this to the bank: She is probably also the most voracious learner you know. The biggest mistake that keeps a person from becoming smarter is thinking that being smart is a fixed status, rather than a dynamic process. It's sort of like the mistake overweight people make when looking at thin people: The overweight person might remark that the thin person is lucky because "he can eat whatever he wants," whereas the thin person knows he is thin precisely because he does NOT eat whatever he wants. The smartest people are the ones who never declare victory over learning.

"Yes, if you are a proactive learner, you will actually know more and more. But as soon as you take what you already know—about anything whatsoever—and declare victory, you will be on the path to being a little bit dumber—and not just about that specific matter. That means letting go of the idea that "being smart" means you already know everything.

"That's why 'proactive learning' is the first key building block for developing critical thinking skills. If you want to be really smart, act like you don't know anything and go from there. That's the first step to proactive learning: Keep an open mind. Then you will have lots of space to store a regular stream of new information, technique, and perspective. Study information and you will build your stored knowledge base. Practice technique and you will build your stored skill base. Contemplate different perspectives and you will build stored wisdom. Never declare victory. Keep learning.

"No matter how smart you are, if you are in the habit of proactive learning, you will keep getting smarter. That's what makes proactive learning the ultimate transferable skill. And, unlike the hot technical skills, it will never become obsolete."

Proactive Learning: Lesson Plan 1—Proactive Learning

Step One *Consider the following statement:* "Proactive learning is the first key to become a critical thinker."

Brainstorming questions: What does "proactive learning" mean to you? Can you think of specific examples? Why is proactive learning important? Why is it in the best interests of this organization—your current employer—to have employees who are committed to proactive learning? Why is it in your best interests as an employee to be committed to proactive learning? Are there downsides or good reasons to NOT be committed to proactive learning?

Step Two Make a list of the subjects or areas inside or outside of work where you do the most proactive learning. What have you learned? How did you learn it? What did you actually do, step by step, in doing that proactive learning? Are you still in learning mode? What are you learning? How? What are you actually doing, step by step?

Step Three *Consider the following paragraph:* Knowledge work is NOT about what you do, but rather, it is about HOW you do whatever you do. Any task/responsibility/project is knowledge work if you leverage skill, knowledge, and wisdom in accomplishing it.

> *FOR EXAMPLE: Even if you are digging a ditch, there is skill, knowledge, and wisdom you can leverage. What is the best way to grip the shovel? What is the most effective technique for striking the ground? What is the most effective technique for lifting the dirt? What kind of shovel should you use? What kind of gloves? What is the best physical posture? What is the best pace?*

Brainstorm: Take a moment to clarify for yourself the precise meaning of skill, knowledge, and wisdom.

Skill (the mastery of technique). List examples:

Knowledge (the master of information). List examples:

Wisdom (the understanding of many, many perspectives). List examples:

Step Four   Now make a list of your tasks, responsibilities, and projects at work.

Take them one at a time. For each, ask yourself: Do some of them seem more to you like knowledge work, while other seem less like knowledge work? Which ones seem like knowledge work? Why? Which ones do not? Why?

Again, take them one at a time. For each, now consider: In doing this task/responsibility/project, what can you do to leverage more skill, knowledge, and wisdom in order to do a better job? From what source could you gain that learning?

Step Five   At work, think of something about which you are really excited to learn more. Choose one of your tasks/responsibilities/projects above for which you could really benefit from doing some proactive learning. Now make a proactive learning plan.

LEARNING PLAN
First, spell out your learning goals and assess your available resources.

♦ Make a list of knowledge you want to master. What information do you need? From what sources? What resources are available?

♦ Make a list of skills you want to master. What techniques do you need? From what sources? What resources are available?

◆ Make a list of the wisdom you wish to acquire. What perspectives do you need? From what sources? What resources are available?

Second, set concrete goals for yourself with a reasonable deadline and any guidelines or specifications.

Goals Guidelines	Specifications Intermediate Goals	Deadlines

Third, for each goal, spell out a list of intermediate goals and deadlines.

Then, for each intermediate goal/deadline, spell out your concrete learning actions. For example:

◆ *Research:* Seek out information, technique, and/or perspective.
◆ *Vet sources:* Compare different sources and try to choose the best sources.
◆ *Organize:* Organize the raw information, technique, and perspective.
◆ *Learn:* Study the information until it turns into stored knowledge; practice the techniques until they turn into stored skills; or contemplate the perspectives until they turn into stored wisdom.

Step Six   HOMEWORK OPTION. Go ahead and execute that learning plan!

Proactive Learning: Lesson Plan 2—Open Mind

Step One   *Consider the following statement:* "Keeping an open mind is the first key to proactive learning."

Brainstorming questions: What does "keeping an open mind" mean to you? Can you think of specific examples? Why is keeping an open mind important to proactive learning?

Step Two   *Consider the following:* Let's assume closed-mindedness is the opposite of open-mindedness.

Brainstorming questions: What does "closed-mindedness" mean to you? Can you think of specific examples? Why does closed-mindedness get in the way of proactive learning?

Step Three   Make a list of at least ten statements about which you are absolutely certain.

Step Four   Now take them one at a time. For each one, ask yourself:

- Why are you so sure?
- What assumptions are you making that have not been proven?
- What do you really know about this matter?
- What is your source of information?
- How much have you really investigated?
- What would it take for you to second-guess this statement?
- What would it take to change your mind?
- What would it take to prove you wrong about this?
- What if the opposite is true? What else must be true in order for this "opposite" to be true? Construct the strongest argument you can to prove the "opposite" statement:
- What facts would be necessary?
- What are the best reasons to consider the "opposite" statement?
- What are the best reasons to believe the "opposite" statement?

Step Five   HOMEWORK OPTION. Choose at least one of the "opposite" statements above to research and prove true. Start with the list of "facts" that would be necessary for the "opposite" statement to be true. For each of those facts, ask yourself:

- What sources of information could confirm those facts?
- How can I access those sources of information?
- Where should I begin?

Frame your research inquiry, fact by fact:

What Sources?	Steps to Access Source	Start Here	FACTS

Once you've done your research, write out an argument to prove your case. The key to framing a good argument is making very good use of the word "because."

FRAMEWORK FOR MAKING A GOOD ARGUMENT

Assertion/conclusion:

. . . is true *because* . . .

Fact/source, which is important *because*. . .

. . . if this fact is true, these other facts cannot be true. . .

OR

. . . if this fact is true, these other facts must also be true. . .

Fact/source, which is important because. . .

. . . if this fact is true, these other facts cannot be true. . .

OR

. . . if this fact is true, these other facts must also be true . . .

Fact/source, which is important because . . .

. . . if this fact is true, these other facts cannot be true . . .

OR

. . . if this fact is true, these other facts must also be true . . .

The more facts and sources, of course, the stronger the argument.

Proactive Learning: Lesson Plan 3—Suspend Judgment, Question Assumptions, and Seek to Learn

Step One   *Consider the following statement:* "Keeping an open mind" means suspending judgment, questioning assumptions, and seeking to learn.

Brainstorming questions:

- What does "suspending judgment" mean to you? Can you think of specific examples? Why is "suspending judgment" an important part of keeping an open mind?
- What does "questioning assumptions" mean to you? Can you think of specific examples? Why is "questioning assumptions" an important part of keeping an open mind?
- What does "seeking to learn" mean to you? Can you think of specific examples? Why is "seeking to learn" an important part of keeping an open mind?

Step Two   Make a list of your current tasks, responsibilities and projects at work.

Step Three   Take your tasks, responsibilities and projects, one by one. For each one, consider this question: When performing this task/responsibility/project, what are the key moments when it would be really helpful to keep an open mind?

Step Four   For each of those key moments, try using the mantra of "open mindedness":

- Suspend judgment
- Question assumptions
- Seek to learn

For each, ask yourself:

- Do I have a clear picture in my head?
- What parts of the picture seem the most clear?

- Are those clear parts of the picture, in fact, untested assumptions?
- How can I test those assumptions?

Interrogate every single assumption:

- How do I know that?
- What is my source of information?
- Is that a reliable source? Is there another source?
- Does it fit with common sense?
- Does it fit with everything else I know? Am I sure? How sure am I?

The reason to question assumptions is to figure out what you don't know for sure so you can be clear about what you need to learn.

Proactive Learning: Lesson Plan 4—Question Assumptions

Step One   Make a list of your current tasks, responsibilities, and projects at work.

Step Two   Take your tasks, responsibilities, and projects, one by one. For each one, ask yourself:

- ◆ What do you know about this task/responsibility/project? Make a list of everything you know about it and how you know what you know.
- ◆ What assumptions are you making? What can you do to check your assumptions? What else can you learn?
- ◆ What don't you know about this task/responsibility/project? Make a list of everything you don't know and what sources of information might hold the answers.
- ◆ What can you do to start tapping those sources and filling in those gaps in your knowledge.

Step Three   HOMEWORK OPTION. Choose one of your tasks, responsibilities, or projects from your list above – choose one about which you want to do some proactive learning.

Start with your list of everything you think you know and double-check every single fact. See what you find.

Now take the list of everything you do not know and your preliminary list of sources. One by one, source by source, go find the answers.

Pay close attention to what you learn!

Proactive Learning: Lesson Plan 5—Research

Step One   Research can be defined as "identifying and defining information needs so as to ask the right questions and then gathering good information from reliable sources quickly to find accurate and useful answers to those questions."

- What experiences have you had conducting research (at work, in school, or in your personal life)?
- When have you conducted research on a subject? What subject?
- What steps did you follow? What did you learn?
- What did you learn from that experience about the process of research itself? If you had to design a research project now on another topic, what steps would you follow?

Step Two   Remember the distinctions among knowledge, skill, and wisdom:

- Knowledge comes from studying good information.
- Skill comes from practicing good technique.
- Wisdom comes from appreciating and understanding multiple perspectives.

Brainstorm: What different research tactics might one use for researching "information" to build knowledge versus "technique" to build skill versus "perspective" to build wisdom? What different sources might one use for researching "information" versus "technique" versus "wisdom"?

Step Three   *Consider this:* The first key to research is asking good questions.
   Brainstorm: Consider the following elements of a good research question:

- Relevant to something that is of interest or concern
- Open-ended but not too open
- Focused but not too closed

- Narrow enough in scope that it can be answered in the time available
- Clear
- Evident questions: who, where, when
- Less evident questions: why, how, what

Brainstorm: What other elements might be important to a good research question?

Brainstorm: How might one's research questions differ when it comes to "information" versus "technique" versus "perspective"?

Step Four *Consider this:* The second key to research is finding good sources to answer one's research questions:

Brainstorm: Consider the following elements of a good source:

- Proven expertise based on experience, education, or research
- Validated and recognized by independent third parties
- Facts are clearly distinguished from opinions
- Facts are not merely asserted, but include explanations for how they were determined
- Facts make sense in terms of other demonstrable facts
- When facts diverge from other demonstrable facts, that is acknowledged and explained
- Alternative facts and arguments are acknowledged and explained

Brainstorm: What other elements might be important in a good source?

Brainstorm: How might one's best sources differ when it comes to "information" versus "technique" versus "perspective"?

Step Five Make a list of your current tasks, responsibilities, and projects at work. Now choose one for which you would benefit from doing some research. Choose one about which you would be excited to do some research. Make a research plan:

The first key: Write your research questions.

What is the primary, overall question you want to answer?

Now break it down:

♦ Are you seeking knowledge, skill, or wisdom?
♦ What other questions will you need to answer along the way?
♦ Who
♦ Where
♦ When
♦ Why
♦ How
♦ What
♦ What else?

The second key: Identify the best sources to answer your questions.
For your primary question, what are the best sources?
Now break it down:

♦ For each of the questions along the way, what is the best source?
♦ What sources have proven expertise?
♦ What sources are validated by independent third parties?
♦ What facts do you need?
♦ What opinions do you need?
♦ Do the facts make sense?
♦ Are they in alignment with consensus?
♦ Are they divergent?
♦ Do they make logical arguments?
♦ Do they acknowledge and explain other divergent facts and arguments?

Make the plan:

Goals	Intermediate Goals	Step-by-Step Checklist

Step Six HOMEWORK OPTION. Go ahead and execute that research plan!

Proactive Learning: Lesson Plan 6—Study Skills— Building Knowledge

Step One   Think of something you know a lot about.

Brainstorming questions: What do you know about the subject? Make a list of what you know. How do you know it? What did you study? When did you study? Where did you study? With whom did you study? How did you study? What steps did you follow?

Step Two   Consider the following study skills:

- *Memorization:* Think of something you have memorized in the past. Do you still remember it? What is it? When did you memorize it? Where? With whom? How? What steps did you follow?
- *Summarizing lessons from reading/listening:* Think of something you have read or listened to in the past from which you have learned something valuable. Can you summarize what you learned? What did you read or to whom did you listen? When? Where? How did you go about learning what you learned? What steps did you follow?

Step Three   Make a list of your current tasks, responsibilities, and projects at work. Now take them one by one and ask yourself the following questions:

- What additional knowledge would really benefit you in the performance of that task/responsibility/project?
- What information would be really valuable to memorize?
- What information would be really valuable to read or listen to and be able to summarize some concrete lessons?
- What is a good source from which to get that information?

Step Four   Choose one of those valuable pieces of information to memorize. Preferably it should be a piece of information that would be fun to memorize and useful to know by heart.

- Make a study sheet: Write down all the information you want to memorize.
- Take it one piece at a time.

- Read it. Close your eyes and try to recall it from memory.
- Learn the second piece the same way.
- Then try to remember the first piece, the second piece . . . and learn the third piece.
- Then the first, second, third . . . and learn the fourth. And so on.
- Once you know it by heart, start using it. Keep using it.

Once you finish, choose something else that would be fun to memorize and useful to know by heart. And another. And so on.

Step Five HOMEWORK OPTION. Choose one of those valuable pieces of information that would be good to learn from and summarize lessons. Once you finish, choose something else. And another. And so on.

Proactive Learning: Lesson Plan 7—Practice Skills—Building Skill

Step One　Think of something you know how to do very well—a skill.

Brainstorming questions: What skills do you have in this area? What do you know how to do?

Make a list. How did you learn this skill? What did you practice? When did you practice? Where did you practice? With whom did you practice? How did you practice? What steps did you follow?

Step Two　Consider the following practice skills:

◆ *Understand a technique:* A technique is a precise sequence of steps with defined specifications. First, you have to understand the sequence and the specifications before you can try following the sequence. Can you think of a technique you had to learn? Think about when you first learned it. Before you could practice, you had to understand, right? Understanding comes first.

◆ *Practice the technique:* Once you know what you are trying to do, you can start trying to do it. Usually practicing a precise sequence of steps with defined specifications is awkward in the initial attempts. Repetition is the key. Think of a technique you are good at. Think about when you first tried doing it. At first it was awkward, right? Repetition is the key to success.

◆ *Getting so used to the technique, it becomes a habit:* Once you do a technique enough times, it becomes a habit. You do it without even thinking about it. That's when you have to be really careful. If you go on autopilot, almost always, your skill will diminish a little bit at a time without you even noticing it. Have you ever had the experience of going on autopilot with a skill that has become a habit? Did you lose interest or have a time when you started making more mistakes? What did you learn from that experience?

◆ *No matter how much you are in the habit, keep trying to get better:* There is always room for improvement. The key to staying engaged and successful is to keep trying to get better. Have you had the experience of getting better and better and better at something? What was it? What did you learn from that?

Step Three   Make a list of your current tasks, responsibilities, and projects at work. Now take them one by one and ask yourself the following questions:

- What additional skill would really benefit you in the performance of that task/responsibility/project?
- What techniques would be really valuable to understand and practice?
- What is a good source from which to get those techniques?

Step Four   Choose one of those valuable techniques to practice. Preferably it should be a technique that would be fun to practice and useful to be good at.

- Lay out the technique in a precise sequence of steps with defined specifications.
- Make sure you understand the precise sequence and the defined specifications.
- Try doing it. Let it be awkward.
- Do it again. And again.
- Check what you are doing against the precise sequence and the defined specifications. Break it down. Check each step. Check each specification.
- Correct your own technique.
- Do it again and again and again.
- Ask someone who is really good at it to check your technique and make corrections.
- Do it again and again and again.
- Don't stop trying to get better.

Once you finish, choose another skill to practice. And then another. And so on.

Step Five   HOMEWORK OPTION. Keep practicing!

Proactive Learning: Lesson Plan 8—Contemplate Competing Perspectives to Build Wisdom

Step One   Think of something about which you have some real wisdom.

Brainstorming questions: What do you understand and appreciate about the subject? Make a list of what you understand and appreciate. How many perspectives do you understand?

List all the different perspectives you can about this matter. For each one, describe the perspective:

◆ How do you know it?
◆ Where did you learn it?
◆ When?
◆ From what source? With whom?
◆ What differentiates this perspective from other perspectives?
◆ What is legitimate about this perspective? What is problematic about it?

Step Two   Consider the following contemplation skills:

◆ First, you have to take in the perspective and understand it. That means summarizing lessons from reading/listening: Think of something you have read or listened to in the past from which you have learned something valuable. Can you summarize what you learned? What did you read or to whom did you listen? When? Where? How did you go about learning what you learned? What steps did you follow?

◆ Next, you want to understand the argument underlying the perspective. Learn the argument and be able to restate it. Remember a good argument follows this pattern:
  Assertion/conclusion:
  . . . is true because . . .
  Fact/source, which is important because . . .
  . . . if this fact is true, these other facts cannot be true . . .
  OR
  . . . if this fact is true, these other facts must also be true . . .
  + Fact/source, + Fact/source, etc.

- Once you understand the argument, interrogate the argument by asking a bunch of challenging questions.
- Then seek out a very different perspective on the same subject and go through the process above.
- Then another very different perspective and another and another.

Step Three   Make a list of your current tasks, responsibilities, and projects at work. Now take them one by one and ask yourself the following questions: What additional wisdom would really benefit you in the performance of that task/responsibility/project? What differing perspectives would be really valuable to understand? What are good sources from which to get differing perspectives?

Step Four   Choose one of those valuable pieces of wisdom. Preferably it should be a matter that would be fun to contemplate and useful to really understand better.

- Make a list of sources from which you can find differing perspectives.
- Take the sources one by one:
    Summarize the lessons.
    Outline the argument.
    Interrogate the argument.
    Think about it.
- Think about the different perspectives in relation to each other.

Once you finish this process, choose something else and do it again. And another. And so on.

How to Teach Problem Solving

Problem solving: Mastering established best practices—proven repeatable solutions for dealing with regular recurring problems—so as to avoid reinventing the wheel. Using repeatable solutions to improvise when addressing problems that are new but similar.

THE GAP

> *Manager:* "When unexpected problems arise, they don't know how to respond. They can't just find the answer on their cell phones. Half the time they just freeze up. I guess that's better than doing something really stupid, which is what happens the other half."

> *Gen Zer:* "If it is an unexpected problem, then I'm going to try to find a manager to tell me what to do. If I can't find someone, then I need to make a judgment call. What else am I supposed to do? I can't help it if he doesn't agree with my judgment call."

THE BRIDGE: WHAT YOU, THE MANAGER, NEED TO REMEMBER

It may well be true that today's information environment, in which there are so many answers to so many questions available at the tip of their fingers, many young people today are simply not in the habit of thinking on their feet. Without a lot of experience puzzling through problems, it should be no surprise that Gen Zers are often puzzled when they encounter unanticipated problems.

Here's the thing: Nine out of ten times, you don't want your youngest, least experienced employees on the front lines to make important decisions on the basis of their own judgment anyway, especially not if they could instead rely on the accumulated experience of the organization.

The reality is that most of the problems new, young employees are likely to encounter in the workplace should not require them to make judgment calls. Most of the problems they encounter are probably regularly recurring problems—even though the young employee in question may have no experience with the particular problem at hand. Nonetheless, the problem has occurred before and been solved before, probably many times over. Very few of the problems they encounter should be difficult to anticipate.

Think about it: How many problems do your new, young employees encounter that haven't already been solved before?

The key to teaching anybody the basics of problem solving is to teach them to anticipate the most common recurring problems and prepare them with ready-made solutions. First, they will become familiar with commonly recurring problems and therefore be more likely to try to help prevent those problems and also be less often surprised when those problems do arise. Second, they will build up a repertoire of ready-made solutions so there will be problems they can solve without having to chase anybody down. They will have the solution right there in their back pockets. Third, from learning and implementing ready-made solutions, they will learn a lot about the anatomy of a good solution. This will put them in a much better position to borrow from ready-made solutions and improvise a better solution when they do encounter the rare unanticipated problem.

Ready-made solutions are just best practices that have been captured, turned into standard operating procedures, and deployed throughout the organization to employees for use as job aids. The most common job aid is a simple checklist:

If A happens, you do B.
If C happens, you do D.
If E happens, you do F.

What kind of job aids do you have at your disposal to help your new, young employees master best practices for dealing with recurring problems, so they don't have to "problem solve" anew each time? If you already have such job aids at your disposal, then how can you make better use of them as learning tools? You need to have everybody using those tools. Use them to help your young employees (and probably those of all ages) to anticipate and prepare for the most common problems, to build up their repertoires of ready-made solutions, and to learn the anatomy of a good solution so they are in a better position to improvise when there is truly a judgment call.

TEACHING/LEARNING OBJECTIVE

Help them learn better problem-solving skills by teaching them to anticipate regularly recurring problems and master proven ready-made solutions to those problems.

MAKE THEM AWARE/MAKE THEM CARE

Your script: "Here's why you should care of about getting really good at problem solving: Problems are bad. They cost time, energy, and money, and they often leave people—including you—with negative feelings. Even small problems are bad because they often hide and fester and grow and later turn into bigger problems.

"The good news is that most of the problems you will encounter at work are not new problems, no matter how unfamiliar they may be to you. Most of the problems you will encounter are problems that have occurred and been solved many times before. That means we already have the ready-made solutions. All you have to do is learn them.

"Ready-made solutions are simply best practices that have been captured and turned into standard operating procedures so that employees are better prepared to address regularly recurring problems. These tools are very common in workplaces where problems can be very dangerous and where there is very little tolerance for error: battlefields, hospitals, airplane cockpits, nuclear weapons launch sites, and so on.

"By learning and practicing ready-made step-by-step solutions, one after another, you will develop a growing list of problems for which you are well prepared with a growing repertoire of solutions. Solving problems with proven best practices is the best way to gain experience in solving problems successfully. Not only that, but by preparing in advance for regularly recurring problems, you will also be in a much better position to anticipate when those problems might occur and possibly prevent or avoid a problem altogether.

"Here's the really good news: You will become better not only at solving the specific problems anticipated, but also you will be much better at solving unanticipated problems. Why is that? By learning to implement specific step-by-step solutions to recurring problems, you will learn a lot about what good problem solving looks like—like so many case studies. You will begin to understand and appreciate the common denominators and underlying principles. Over time, you will learn how to draw on those common denominators and underlying principles when facing unanticipated problems. You might draw on elements of ready-made solutions, even mixing and matching, to come up with solutions to unanticipated problem should the need arise to improvise."

Problem Solving: Lesson Plan 1—Introduction

Step One   *Brainstorm:* What does "problem solving" mean to you?

Step Two   *Brainstorm:* Think of a time—inside or outside of work—when you have successfully solved a problem. What was the problem? What was the solution? How did you arrive at the solution? When did this happen? Where? Who was involved? What steps did you follow? What lesson can you draw from this experience that would help you solve similar problems in the future? What general lessons about problem solving itself can you draw from this experience that would help you solve very different kinds of problems in the future?

Step Three   *Brainstorm:* Think of someone you know—inside or outside of work—whom you consider to be very good at solving problems. Can you think of an example of a problem that you've witnessed this person solving? What was the problem? What was the solution? How did this problem-solver arrive at the solution? When did this happen? Where? Who else was involved? What steps did the problem-solver follow? What lessons can you draw from this experience that would help you solve similar problems in the future? What general lessons about problem-solving itself can you draw from this experience that would help you solve very different kinds of problems in the future?

Step Four   Consider the following definition of problem solving: "Problem solving: Mastering established best practices—proven repeatable solutions for dealing with regular recurring problems—so as to avoid reinventing the wheel. Using repeatable solutions to improvise when addressing problems that are new but similar."

Brainstorming questions: Why is this approach to problem-solving in the best interests of the organization? Why is this approach to problem solving in your best interest as an employee?

Problem Solving: Lesson Plan 2—Preventing or Avoiding Problems Before They Happen

Step One   *Brainstorm:* Make a list of the most common recurring problems that you encounter at work.

Step Two   Now take the problems, one by one. For each one, answer the following questions:

- When does this problem typically occur?
- Where?
- Who is typically involved?
- What happens in the typical instance of this problem?
- How does the problem usually unfold?
- Why does this problem occur?
- Can you think of steps that could be taken to prevent or avoid the problem?

Step Three   Now take the problems again, one by one. For each one, answer the following questions:

- Are there "official" standard operating procedures for preventing or avoiding this problem?
- If there are standard operating procedures for preventing or avoiding this problem: What are the standard operating procedures? Is there a tool, such as a checklist, that contains those standard operating procedures? Do you have the tool? Do you use the tool? What can you do to make better use of it? Can you memorize it?
- If there is no tool, can you make a tool for yourself containing those standard operating procedures so that you can use it going forward?
- If there are no "official" standard operating procedures for preventing or avoiding this problem, then brainstorm: What are the most common "unofficial" approaches you know of? Is there a prevailing approach? Or are there multiple competing approaches? If there are multiple competing approaches, what do you think are the relative merits of the multiple competing approaches? Have you ever taken action to prevent or avoid this problem? If so, what approach did you take? How did it go?

◆ If there are no "official" standard operating procedures for preventing or avoiding this problem, then create some. Brainstorm: What do you think should be the standard operating procedures—step by step— for preventing or avoiding this problem?

Once you've developed a list of proposed standard operating procedures: Can you create a tool containing the standard operating procedures you just developed? What can you do to make sure you make good use of this tool going forward?

Step Four　What regularly occurring problems can you anticipate encountering in the coming days and weeks at work? What can you do to prepare in advance so that you can help avoid or prevent the problem from occurring?

Step Five　HOMEWORK OPTION. Choose one of the standard operating procedures and the corresponding tool from above. Consider trying to memorize it. If not, then at least make an effort to use it in the coming days at work. Take notes on your efforts to use it and discuss them with your manager in your next one-on-one.

Problem Solving: Lesson Plan 3—Ready-Made Solutions to Commonly Occurring Problems

Step One   *Brainstorm:* Make a list of the most common recurring problems that you encounter at work.

Step Two   Now take the problems, one by one. For each one, answer the following questions:

- When does this problem typically occur?
- Where?
- Who is typically involved?
- What happens in the typical instance of this problem?
- How does the problem usually unfold?
- Why does this problem occur?

Step Three   Now take the problems again, one by one. For each one, answer the following questions:

- Are there "official" standard operating procedures for solving this problem when it occurs?
- If there are standard operating procedures for solving this problem: What are the standard operating procedures? Is there a tool, such as a checklist, that contains those standard operating procedures? Do you have the tool? Do you use the tool? What can you do to make better use of it? Can you memorize it?
- If there is no tool, can you make a tool for yourself containing those standard operating procedures so that you can use it going forward?
- If there are no "official" standard operating procedures for solving this problem, then brainstorm: What are the most common "unofficial" approaches you know of? Is there a prevailing approach? Or are there multiple competing approaches? If there are multiple competing approaches, what do you think are the relative merits of the multiple competing approaches? Have you ever encountered this problem yourself? How did you solve it? What approach did you take? How did it go?

◆ If there are no "official" standard operating procedures for solving this problem, create some. Brainstorm: What do you think should be the standard operating procedures—step by step—for solving this problem?

◆ Once you've developed a list of proposed standard operating procedures: Can you create a tool containing the standard operating procedures you just developed? What can you do to make sure you make good use of this tool going forward?

Step Four   What regularly occurring problems can you anticipate encountering in the coming days and weeks at work? What can you do to prepare in advance so that you will be ready to solve that problem when/if it occurs?

Step Five   HOMEWORK OPTION. Choose one of the standard operating procedures and the corresponding tool from above. Consider trying to memorize it. If not, then at least make an effort to use it in the coming days at work. Take notes on your efforts to use it and discuss them with your manager in your next one-on-one.

Problem Solving: Lesson Plan 4—Common Denominators and Underlying Principles

Step One   Make a list of the most common recurring problems at work for which you have good standard operating procedures for preventing and/or solving the problem.

Step Two   Now review each set of standard operating procedures, one set at a time. For each one, ask yourself:

- ◆ What are the general principles underlying this standard operating procedure?
- ◆ What do you learn from these general principles?

Keep a running list of general principles as you go through each set of standard operating procedures.

Step Three   Now review carefully the running list of general principles.

- ◆ What are the common denominators? The principles common to multiple sets of standard operating procedures?
- ◆ What do you learn from these common denominators?

Step Four   Now think of some very rarely occurring problems, problems for which there are no standard operating procedures because the problem would be so rare. Consider how you could draw on these general principles, especially the common denominators, in order to confront rarely occurring problems that are more difficult to anticipate.

Step Five   HOMEWORK OPTION. Take that list of general principles, especially the common denominators. Consider trying to memorize it. If not, then at least make an effort to use it in the coming days at work. Apply those general principles to everything you do for a while. Take notes on your efforts to use it and discuss them with your manager in your next one-on-one.

Problem Solving: Lesson Plan 5—Applying the After Action Review Tool

Step One   Make a list of some real problems you've encountered at work – the more recent the better.

Step Two   Take those problems one by one. For each one, please complete what's known as an "after action" review:

What actually happened, step by step?

When	Who	What	Where	How	Why

What actions did you take to try to avoid or prevent the problem? Why? What was the outcome?

Actions	Why?	Outcome?

What actions did you take to try to solve the problem? Why? What was the outcome?

Actions	Why?	Outcome

What were the leading alternative actions you could have taken to avoid or prevent the problem that were not taken? What different outcomes might have occurred?

Alternative Actions	Possible Different Outcomes

What were the leading alternative actions you could have taken to solve the problem that were not taken? What different outcomes might have occurred?

Alternative Actions	Possible Different Outcomes

Step Three   Consider the after-action reviews. What do you learn from this? How can you improve?

Step Four HOMEWORK. Consider using an after-action review tool going forward to analyze future problems when you encounter them so at least you can learn from them. If you do use the tool going forward, discuss what you learn in your one-on-one conversations with your manager.

Problem Solving: Lesson Plan 6—Using the After–Action Review Tool to Learn from Others

Step One   Make a list of some heroic problem solving cases you know of at work—the more recent the better.

Step Two   Take these heroic problem solving cases one by one. For each one, please complete what's known as an "after action" review:
    What actually happened, step by step?

When	Who	What	Where	How	Why

What actions were taken to try to avoid or prevent the problem? Why? What were the outcomes?

Actions	Why?	Outcome

What actions were taken to try to solve the problem? Why? What was the outcome?

Actions	Why?	Outcome

Really try to break it down and spell it out so you can see exactly what actions led to the heroic problem solving.

What were the leading alternative actions that could have been taken that might have led to a less heroic outcome? What different outcomes might have occurred?

Alternative Actions	Possible Different Outcomes

Step Three   Consider the after-action reviews. What do you learn from these cases of heroic problem solving? What are the general principles? What are the common denominators?

How to Teach Decision Making

Decision making: Identifying and considering multiple options, assessing the pros and cons of each, and choosing the course of action closest to the desired outcome.

THE GAP

> *Manager:* "No matter how many problems we can help them anticipate and prepare for in advance, there are going to be times when they have to apply some independent judgment and make a decision. But they have so little real-world experience to inform their judgments."

> *Gen Zer:* "My mom has the best judgment of anyone I know, so she's usually who I would call if I had to make a tough decision."

THE BRIDGE: WHAT YOU, THE MANAGER, NEED TO REMEMBER

Participants in our seminars sometimes ask me why I draw a distinction between "problem solving" and "decision making." Indeed, decision making could be seen as a very advanced form of problem solving. But I like to shine a bright light on this distinction: Nine out of ten problems people face in the workplace—especially the problems new, young employees face—have been solved already. So usually the best way to solve a problem is to take a good, repeatable solution from the past and apply it in the moment. That's why my approach to problem solving is nine-tenths about capturing and learning repeatable solutions so as to prepare in advance for the recurring problem. Decision making, on the other hand, is for that rare breed of problem—or that sliver present in every problem—when the decision has not been made already by someone with more experience and authority.

Think about that sliver of any problem when one has to decide what the problem really is in the first place.

What is the essence of decision making anyway? It's not the same thing as sheer brain power, mental capacity, or natural intelligence. It's not a matter of accumulated knowledge or memorized information. It is more than the mastery of techniques and tools.

If you think of decision making, perhaps you think of the most basic decision-making tool, the weighing of pros and cons. But pros and cons are really just predictions of likely outcomes. So your pros and cons list is useless if you can't accurately predict the likely outcomes of one choice versus another.

Good decision making is really about being able to predict likely outcomes—the ability to see the connections between cause and effect—to project out the consequences of one set of events and actions, as opposed to another. The irony is that the only way to develop that "go forward" ability to predict the future is to learn from the past.

I recall witnessing a Gen Zer, maybe sixteen or seventeen, going through a brunch buffet line. She turned to her mother and asked, "Mom, do I like scrambled eggs?" Her mother turned to her and said, "Well, you've had scrambled eggs before." The young lady said, "I know. Did I like them?"

Experience alone does not teach good decision making. The key to learning from experience is paying close attention and aggressively drawing lessons from one's experiences. If you can begin to see the patterns in causes and their effects, then you can start to think ahead with insight. Ultimately, that's the key to decision-making.

TEACHING/LEARNING OBJECTIVE
Help them learn better decision-making skills by teaching them to identify and consider multiple options, assess the pros and cons of each, and choose the course of action closest to the desired outcome.

MAKE THEM AWARE/MAKE THEM CARE
Your script: "Here's why you should care about becoming really good at decision making: Decision making is a very high-level skill that is very hard to develop without years of experience. But you can accelerate the learning curve. "The key is learning to understand the connection between cause and effect so that you can learn to predict the future. How does it work?

"In retrospect, the key is working backward from effects to assess likely causes, to figure out what decisions and actions led to the current situation. That means being really aggressive about learning from your own experiences.

"This is the essence of the lessons-learned process that is ubiquitous in the military and intelligence agencies. Every mission is subjected to intense scrutiny immediately after the fact. Leaders at all levels involved in a mission are expected to go over every decision and action, step by step, to determine exactly what happened and why. Then they meet to discuss and debate these decisions and actions. They call it an after-action review.

"You want to learn to apply this process to every 'mission' you undertake at work, to every move you make at work: Do you stop and reflect after making decisions and taking actions? Do you stop and reflect on outcomes and consequences? Do you look at outcomes and consequences and trace them back to see the chains of cause and effect? What actually happened, step by step? What decisions were made? What actions were taken? What different outcomes might have occurred?

"Going forward, the key to becoming good at decision making is learning to think ahead and accurately project the likely outcomes and consequences of specific decisions and actions.

"Have you ever played chess or any other game of strategy? The key to success in any game of strategy is thinking ahead. Before making a move, you play out in your head the likely outcomes, often over a long sequence of moves and countermoves. If I do A, the other player would probably respond with B. Then I would do C, and he would probably respond with D. Then I would do E, and he would probably respond with F. And so on. This is what strategic planners call a decision/action tree because each decision or action is the beginning of a branch of responses and counter-responses. In fact, each decision or action creates a series of possible responses, and each possible response creates a series of possible counter-responses.

"You want to learn to think ahead and play out the likely sequence of moves and countermoves in everything you do: Do you think about cause and effect? Do you stop and reflect before making decisions and taking actions? Do you project likely outcomes in advance? Do you look at each decision and action as a set of choices, each with identifiable consequences?"

Decision Making: Lesson Plan 1—Introduction

Step One   *Brainstorm:* What does "decision making" mean to you?

Step Two   *Brainstorm:* Think of a time—inside or outside of work—when you have made a good decision. What was the decision? What were your options? How did you weigh the competing options? Ultimately, how did you make your decision? What were the outcomes/consequences? When did this happen? Where? Who was involved? What steps did you follow? What lesson can you draw from this experience that would help you make good decisions in the future?

Step Three   *Brainstorm:* Think of a time—inside or outside of work—when you have made a decision that turned out to be a bad one. What was the decision? What were your options? How did you weigh the competing options? Ultimately, how did you make your decision? What were the outcomes/consequences? When did this happen? Where? Who was involved? What steps did you follow? What lesson can you draw from this experience that would help you avoid making bad decisions like this one in the future?

Step Four   *Brainstorm:* Think of someone you know—inside or outside of work—whom you consider to be very good at making decisions. Can you think of an example of a decision you've witnessed this person making? What was the decision? What were the competing options? Ultimately, how did this person make the decision? What were the outcomes/consequences? When did this happen? Where? Who else was involved? What steps did the decision-maker follow? What lessons can you draw from this experience that would help you make good decisions in the future?

Step Five   *Brainstorm:* Think of someone you know—inside or outside of work—whom you consider to make bad decisions. Can you think of an example of a decision you've witnessed this person making? What was the decision? What were the competing options? Ultimately, how did this person make the decision? What were the outcomes/consequences? When did this happen? Where? Who else was involved? What steps did the decision-maker follow? What lessons can you draw from this experience that would help you avoid making bad decisions in the future?

Step Six   Consider the following definition of decision making:

"*Decision making:* Identifying and considering multiple options, assessing the pros and cons of each, and choosing the course of action closest to the desired outcome."

Brainstorming questions: Why is this approach to decision making in the best interests of the organization? Why is this approach to decision making in your best interest as an employee?

Decision Making: Lesson Plan 2—Information Analysis: Simple Pros and Cons

Step One   *Brainstorm:* Think of an important decision that you need to make—inside or outside of work. Or else take one of the choice sets below and use that "decision" to be made as your case study. In each of the following choice sets, imagine you must make a mutually exclusive decision: If you could only choose one or the other, would you rather:

- Be paid more money or have more time off?
- Disappoint an important customer or disappoint an important vendor?
- Impress your boss or impress your direct reports?
- Improve the quality of your work or improve your productivity?
- Improve the quality of our products or lower the price?
- Love your work or win prestigious accolades for your work?

Or think of another choice set to use as your example for the following steps.

Step Two   Now consider the decision to be made and the options before you:

- What do you know? What don't you know?
- What else should you know in order to make a good decision?
- Do you need to do some research before considering your options?
  - If so, what are your research questions? and
  - What are your best sources for answering those questions?

Step Three   Now before considering your options, consider what's at stake in making this decision. Answer these questions:

- Why is a decision required?
- When does the decision have to be made?
- What are your goals in making the decision?

- Who else will/might be affected by the decision?
- Who stands to gain? Who stands to lose?
- What rules/principles should you follow in making the decision?

Step Four   Now consider your options. List all of your options. What are all the logical possibilities in this situation?

Step Five   Take all of your options, one by one. For each option, start by making an exhaustive pros and cons list. Of course, not all pros and cons are of the same weight. Take note.

Step Six   Now, for each option, make the strongest argument in favor and the strongest argument against.

Remember a good argument follows this pattern:

Assertion/conclusion:

. . . is true *because* . . .

Fact/source, which is important *because* . . .

. . . if this fact is true, these other facts cannot be true . . .

OR

. . . if this fact is true, these other facts must also be true . . .

+ Fact/source, + Fact/source, and so on.

Step Seven   What are your strongest options? Make a decision.

Decision Making: Lesson Plan 3—Cause and Effect: Positive Outcomes

Step One   *Brainstorm:* Make a list of positive outcomes and consequences that you encounter at work. Consider examples of:

- Happy customers
- Happy employees
- Happy vendors
- Delivering services or products
- Adding value by making things smarter, faster, or better
- Solving problems
- Identifying opportunities
- Making money
- Feeling useful

Step Two   Now take your list of positive outcomes/consequences at work, one by one. For each one, please answer the following questions:

- What causes this positive outcome/consequence?
  - Who is involved?
  - When does it happen?
  - How?
  - Where?
  - What happens?
  - Why does it happen?

Step Three   Again, take the positive outcomes/consequences one by one. For each one, tell the story based on the answers to the questions above. What is the story of how that positive outcome/consequence came to be?

Step Four   Again, for each of the positive outcomes/consequences: What decisions were made along the way? Who made those decisions? What options did the decision-maker have? How could a different decision have resulted in a less positive outcome/consequence?

Step Five   What lessons can you learn from this?

Decision Making: Lesson Plan 4—Cause and Effect: Negative Outcomes

Step One *Brainstorm:* Make a list of negative outcomes and consequences that you might encounter at work. Consider examples of:

- ◆ Unhappy customers
- ◆ Unhappy employees
- ◆ Unhappy vendors
- ◆ Failing to deliver on services or products
- ◆ Making errors in work or failing to get enough done
- ◆ Causing problems
- ◆ Missing opportunities
- ◆ Losing money
- ◆ Feeling bad about the role you play at work

Step Two Now take your list of negative outcomes/consequences at work, one by one. For each one, answer the following questions:

- ◆ What causes this negative outcome/consequence?
  - • Who is involved?
  - • When does it happen?
  - • How?
  - • Where?
  - • What happens?
  - • Why does it happen?

Step Three Again, take the negative outcomes/consequences one by one. For each one, tell the story based on the answers to the questions above. What is the story of how that negative outcome/consequence came to be?

Step Four Again, for each of the negative outcomes/consequences: What decisions were made along the way? Who made those decisions? What options did the decision-maker have? How could a different decision have resulted in a more positive outcome/consequence?

Step Five What lessons do you learn from this? What causes should be avoided? What decisions should not be made?

Decision Making: Lesson Plan 5—Applying the After-Action Review Tool

Step One   Make a list of some real decisions you have encountered at work—the more recent the better.

Step Two   Take those decisions, one by one. For each one, complete an "after-action" review:

What decision was made? Who made it? Why? What was the outcome?

Decisions	Who?	Why?	Outcome

What actions were taken? Who made them? Why? What was the outcome?

Actions	Who?	Why?	Outcome

What were the leading alternative decisions that were not made? What different outcomes might have occurred?

Alternative Decisions	Possible Different Outcomes

What were the leading alternative actions that were not taken? What different outcomes might have occurred?

Alternative Actions	Possible Different Outcomes

Step Three   Consider the after action reviews. What do you learn from this?

Step Four   HOMEWORK. Consider using an after-action review tool going forward to analyze future decisions when you encounter them so you can learn from them. If you do use the tool going forward, discuss what you learn in your one-on-one conversations with your manager.

Decision Making: Lesson Plan 6—Using the Decision/Action Tree

Step One   Make a list of some real decisions you anticipate encountering at work in the coming days or weeks.

Step Two   Take those decisions, one by one. For each one, think ahead:

◆ What are all of your options?

For each option, complete the following decision/action tree:

◆ If you take this decision/action, who is likely to respond, how, when, where, and why?
◆ What set of options will this cut off?
◆ What set of options will this create?

For each option, keep going:
• If you take this decision/action, who is likely to respond, how, when, where, and why?
• What set of options will this cut off?
• What set of options will this create?
For each option, keep going:
• If you take this decision/action, who is likely to respond, how, when, where, and why?
• What set of options will this cut off?
• What set of options will this create?

Step Three   Consider your decision/action trees. What do you learn from this?

Step Four   HOMEWORK. Consider using a decision/action tree going forward to analyze future decisions when you encounter them. If you do use the tool going forward, discuss what you learn in your one-on-one conversations with your manager.

Step Five   HOMEWORK. Get your hands on one or more of the following famous books about strategy:

Sun Tzu's *The Art of War*

Miyamito Mushashi's *The Book of Five Rings*

Nicolo Machiavelli's *The Prince*

HBR's *Must Reads on Strategy*

Read them one by one. For each one, keep a written journal of lessons.

Chapter 6

How to Teach the Missing Basics of Followership to Today's Young Talent

Followership: The Missing Basics

Respect for context: Reading and adapting to the existing structure, rules, customs, and leadership in an unfamiliar situation.

Citizenship: Accepting, embracing, and observing, not just the rights, but the duties of membership/belonging/participation in a defined group with its own structure, rules, customs, and leaders.

Service: Approaching relationships in terms of what you have to offer—respect, commitment, hard work, creativity, sacrifice—rather than what you need or want.

Teamwork: Playing whatever role is needed to support the larger effort; coordinating, cooperating, and collaborating with others in pursuit of a shared goal; celebrating the success of others.

How to Teach Respect for Context

Respect for context: Reading and adapting to the existing structure, rules, customs, and leadership in an unfamiliar situation.

THE GAP

Manager: "They act like we are the ones who should be adapting to them, rather than the other way around. I want to say, 'Listen son, you've been here for twenty days. I've been here for twenty years!'"

> *Gen Zer:* "Let's face it: The past may be yours. But the future is mine. Surely you want me to succeed here, right? What are you going to do to set me up for success?"

THE BRIDGE: WHAT YOU, THE MANAGER, NEED TO REMEMBER

Before any individual can possibly succeed at practicing good "follow-ership," he or she must develop a fundamental respect for context. The person must learn to read and appreciate and accept and embrace adapting to the existing structure, rules, customs, and leaders in an unfamiliar situation.

Indeed, Gen Zers are more likely to disagree openly with employers' missions, policies, and decisions and challenge employment conditions and established reward systems. They are less obedient to employers' rules and supervisors' instructions. They are less likely to heed organizational chart authority. Gen Zers respect transactional authority: control of resources, control of rewards, and control of work conditions. There are really only two ways they can choose to go in a new job: fit in or stand out. Too often, their inclination is to stand out.

Managers often tell us that today's new young employees seem to suffer from a fundamental lack of context. Yes, this is partly a function of youth. Young people have less life experience than older people and thus fewer points of reference to compare circumstances, people, and relationships. Context is all about these points of reference. So lack of context goes with being in the first adult life stages. But there is much more going on here. Our research indicates that Gen Zers have a very particular contextual bias when they enter an established institution with "adult" authority figures. For most Gen Zers, the most familiar context of adult supervision is their experience with parents and teachers and counselors—adult authority figures in highly supportive caretaking roles.

In fact, Gen Zers very much appreciate and respect age and experience. After all, they have been the beneficiaries of an extraordinary level of nurturing in their relationships with adults—more than any generation in history. This does not result in a particular deference to authority or acquiescence to established norms and structures. Rather, they are quite accustomed to child-centric contexts in which their feelings, words, and actions have usually been accorded a huge amount of attention by adult authority figures. Their relationships with adult authority figures have largely been defined in terms of the dedication, commitment, and service of the adults toward the children, not the other way around. Their preferences have been given much weight, and their opinions have been given much airtime in discussions. Misbehavior has been diagnosed instead of punished. Their accomplishments have been celebrated with glee.

As a result, Gen Zers enter the workplace with the expectation that they will now be cared for, rather than being ordered around. Of course, the problem is that, in this context, you are paying them, not the other way around.

The good news is that Gen Zers understand transactional relationships. They know what it means to be the customer. They might just have to be reminded that, in this situation, they are not the customers. The employer is the customer. As the manager, you are not claiming to be superior to them in any kind of absolute sense. You are not claiming to be higher on the "food chain" in the cosmos. You just need to make it clear to them:

> *Just in this context: In this role, in this job, in this chain of command in this organization. I'm the leader. You are the follower. If you want to belong here, this is how you understand, accept, embrace, and adapt to your place in the structure, rules, customs, and leadership here.*

Teaching Gen Zers to develop respect for context means helping them to realize that work is situational and their role in any situation is determined in large part by factors that have nothing to do with them. There are preexisting, independent factors that would be present even if they were not, and these factors determine the context of any situation.

The easiest way to understand context is to consider extreme examples of it: dire illness, hurricanes, war, etc. In any of these contexts, the possibilities are limited, and so is the scope of an individual's potential role. In these contexts, certain expectations, hopes, expressions, and actions are inappropriate. While it is relatively easy to be sensitive to extreme contexts, it is often difficult for people, Gen Zers in particular, to be sensitive to more subtle contexts, particularly when they walk into new situations. Every situation has a context that limits possibilities and limits the scope of an individual's potential role. The big mistake leaders and managers often make is allowing Gen Zers to remain in their vacuum.

The key is making it clear from the outset that, if they want to be set up for success in this situation, they must learn to read and adapt to the existing structure, rules, customs, and leaders.

TEACHING/LEARNING OBJECTIVE

Help them develop respect for context by learning to read and adapt to the existing structure, rules, customs, and leaders in an unfamiliar situation.

MAKE THEM AWARE/MAKE THEM CARE

Your script: "Here's why you should care about learning to read and adapt to a new context—particularly this context.

"No matter who you are, what you want to achieve, or how you want to behave, your role in any work situation is determined in large part by factors that have nothing to do with you. Every situation has a context that limits possibilities and limits the scope of your potential role.

"Once you have a handle on the context of your work situation, next you have to ask yourself where you fit in this context. Why are you here? What is at stake for you? When did you get here? What is your appropriate role in relation to the other people in the group? What is your appropriate role in relation to the mission? What expectations and hopes are reasonable for you to have?

"Once you really understand your role in any work context, then your number one responsibility is to play that role to the absolute best of your ability. That means, contribute your very best, and put in more time and effort no matter how lowly, mundane, or repetitive your tasks and responsibilities might seem in relation to the overall mission of your organization."

Respect for Context: Lesson Plan 1—Introduction

Step One   *Consider:* What does it mean to you to show "respect for context" in an unfamiliar situation?

Step Two   Consider the following definition of "respect for context": "Reading and adapting to the existing structure, rules, customs, and leaders in an unfamiliar situation."
   Brainstorm: Why is this approach to context in the best interests of the organization—your current employer? Why is this approach to context in your best interests as an employee? Are there good reasons to reject this approach to context?

Step Three   Now consider the context of this particular workplace. How can you "read and adapt" to this context? Describe in as much detail as you can:

	Read	Adapt
The structure . . . The rules . . . The customs . . . The leadership . . .		

Respect for Context: Lesson Plan 2—Reading the Structure, Rules, Customs, and Leadership

Step One   Consider the context of this particular workplace. How do you "read" this context? Describe in as much detail as you can:

> The structure . . .
> The rules . . .
> The customs . . .
> The leadership . . .

Step Two   Consider the structure of this workplace. "Read" it.
Brainstorm:

- What do you know?
- What don't you know or understand?
- What do you need to know or understand better?
- How can you learn? What resources and support do you need?

Step Three   Consider the rules of this workplace. "Read" them.
Brainstorm:

- What do you know?
- What don't you know or understand?
- What do you need to know or understand better?
- How can you learn? What resources and support do you need?

Step Four   Consider the customs of this workplace. "Read" them.
Brainstorm:

- What do you know?
- What don't you know or understand?
- What do you need to know or understand better?
- How can you learn? What resources and support do you need?

Step Five   Consider the leadership of this workplace. "Read" it.
Brainstorm:

- ◆ What do you know?
- ◆ What don't you know or understand?
- ◆ What do you need to know or understand better?
- ◆ How can you learn? What resources and support do you need?

Respect for Context: Lesson Plan 3—Where Do You Fit?

Step One *Brainstorm:* Consider the context of this workplace. Where do you "fit" in this context? Ask yourself:

- Where am I? What is this place?
- What is going on here? What is the mission of the group?
- Why is everybody here? What is at stake for the group and for each person in the group?
- When did they all come here?
- Who are all these people? What role does each person play?
- How are they accustomed to doing things around here? What is standard operating procedure?
- Why am I here?
- What is at stake for me?
- When did I come here?
- What is my appropriate role in relation to the other people in the group?
- What is my appropriate role in relation to the mission? Who am I in this context?

Step Two *Brainstorm:* Consider the structure of this workplace. Where do you "fit" in this structure?

Step Three *Brainstorm:* Consider the rules of this workplace. Where do you "fit" in relation to the rules?

Step Four *Brainstorm:* Consider the customs of this workplace. Where do you "fit" in relation to the customs?

Step Five *Brainstorm:* Consider the leadership of this workplace. Where do you "fit" in relation to the leadership in this context?

Respect for Context: Lesson Plan 4—How Can You Adapt?

Step One *Brainstorm:* Consider the overall context of this work place. What do you need to do to "adapt" to this context?

Step Two *Brainstorm:* Consider the structure of this workplace. What do you need to do to adapt to the structure of this workplace?

Step Three *Brainstorm:* Consider the rules of this workplace. What do you need to do to adapt to the rules of this workplace?

Step Four *Brainstorm:* Consider the customs of this workplace. What do you need to do to adapt to the customs of this workplace?

Step Five *Brainstorm:* Consider the leadership of this workplace. What do you need to do to adapt to the leadership of this workplace?

Respect for Context: Lesson Plan 5—Context-Limiting Factors

Step One   Consider each of the following context-limiting factors one by one. For each factor, describe how the factor can shape the context of this workplace:

- Resource constraints—insufficient information, people, material, or tools
- Limited time
- Too much work
- Other people not doing their part
- Things are constantly changing
- Competing priorities
- Distance
- Weather
- Company policies, rules, regulations, and procedures
- The way things have always been done around here
- Too many low priority distractions
- Interruptions
- Conflict between and among employees
- My manager is often unavailable
- Unclear lines of authority
- I answer to too many different people
- Inconsistency from one manager to another

Step Two   Consider each of the factors again, one by one. For each one: Can you think of examples of when you have been in this context? Did you read and adapt to the context well? How could you have read and adapted to the context better?

Step Three   Consider each of the factors again. For each one: Can you anticipate being in this situation again in the future? When is that likely to happen? Where? Who might be involved? What do you think is likely to happen? What options will you have? How will you adapt?

Respect for Context: Lesson Plan 6—Complicated Relationships

Step One   Certain relationship dynamics in the workplace are more complicated than others. Consider the following complicated relationship dynamics:

- The multiple boss problem: Do you answer to more than one boss?
- The chain-of-command problem: Is it clear to you exactly who your immediate boss is?
- Older, more experienced colleagues
- Conflicts, dislikes, and gripes between and among employees
- Friendships, cliques, and other relationships at work
- Interdependency with employees in other teams, departments, or divisions, or outside vendors

List any other complicated relationship dynamics you might have dealt with in the workplace.

Step Two   Consider each of the complicated relationship dynamics one by one. For each one: Can you think of examples of when you have dealt with this dynamic? Did you read and adapt to the context well? How could you have read and adapted to the context better?

Step Three   Consider each of the dynamics again. For each one: Can you anticipate being in this situation again in the future? When is that likely to happen? Where? Who might be involved? What do you think is likely to happen? What options will you have? How will you read and adapt to the context?

Respect for Context: Lesson Plan 7—Positive Contexts

Step One   Consider the following positive workplace contexts:

1. Working primarily on tasks and responsibilities that you enjoy and are particularly good at.
2. Being able to balance your time at work with free time. Rest, recover, relax, and rejuvenate in between times you must work.
3. When you work with people you like and respect. Avoid people you find "toxic" and stick to the ones you appreciate.
4. Working in a workspace that is comfortable and in a location that you enjoy. If only!
5. Leaving your non-work issues at the door when you arrive at work.

Step Two   Consider each of the positive workplace contexts one by one. For each one: Can you think of examples of when you have been in this situation? Did you read and adapt to the context well? How could you have read and adapted to the context even better?

Step Three   Consider the positive contexts again. For each one: Can you anticipate being in this situation again in the future? When is that likely to happen? Where? Who might be involved? What do you think is likely to happen? What options will you have? How will you read and adapt to the context optimally?

Respect for Context: Lesson Plan 8—Negative Contexts

Step One   Consider the following negative workplace contexts:

1. When the work is not necessarily work that you enjoy or excel at
2. When you barely have time to think, much less rest
3. When you have to deal with so many people whom you probably would not choose as your colleagues, including the toxic ones
4. Being physically uncomfortable at work or stuck in a location that is not your preference
5. When things might be problematic in your personal life and it is very hard to leave those issues at the door when you arrive at work

Step Two   Consider each of the negative workplace contexts one by one. For each one: Can you think of examples of when you have been in this situation? Did you read and adapt to the context well? How could you have read and adapted to the context better?

Step Three   Consider the negative contexts again. For each one: Can you anticipate being in this situation again in the future? When is that likely to happen? Where? Who might be involved? What do you think is likely to happen? What options will you have? How will you read and adapt to the context optimally?

Respect for Context: Lesson Plan 9—Dealing with People with Bad Attitudes

Step One   Some people are harder to deal with in the workplace than others. Consider the following "bad attitude" types:

- "Porcupines": Porcupines send the message: "Get away from me!"
- "Entanglers": Entanglers want everybody else to be involved in their issues. They want to be noticed, observed, listened to, and engaged, even if those issues are not the concern of others.
- "Debaters": Debaters always have an argument to make, regardless of whether it is a good argument or not.
- "Complainers": Complainers point out the negatives of a situation without offering a solution.
- "Blamers": Blamers are like complainers, pointing out negatives, but blamers point the finger at a specific individual.
- "Stink bomb throwers": Stink bomb throwers make sarcastic (or worse) remarks, curse under their breath (or aloud), or even make loud gestures such as slamming or yelling.

Step Two   Consider each of the types above. For each one: Can you think of examples of when you have dealt with someone behaving this way? Did you read and adapt to the context well? How could you have read and adapted to the context better?

Step Three   Consider each of the types again. For each one: Can you anticipate being in this situation again in the future? When is that likely to happen? Where? Who might be involved? What do you think is likely to happen? What options will you have? How will you read and adapt to the context?

Respect for Context: Lesson Plan 10—Dealing with People with Great Attitudes

Step One   Some people are much easier to deal with in the workplace than others. Consider the following "great attitude" types:

◆ Someone who is approachable, welcoming, and professional
◆ Someone who communicates in a highly purposeful manner—brief, straightforward, and efficient
◆ Someone who chooses his or her arguments carefully and takes a position based on clear evidence, rather than assertions or opinions
◆ Someone who is a good troubleshooter, placing the focus on what steps can be taken to make things better
◆ Someone who goes out of the way to make positive, optimistic, generous comments, speak in positive tones, and make positive gestures and expressions

Step Two   Consider each of the types above. For each one: Can you think of examples of when you have dealt with someone behaving this way? Did you read and adapt to the context well? How could you have read and adapted to the context better?

Step Three   Consider each of the types again. For each one: Can you anticipate being in this situation again in the future? When is that likely to happen? Where? Who might be involved? What do you think is likely to happen? What options will you have? How will you read and adapt to the context?

How to Teach Good Citizenship

Citizenship: Accepting, embracing, and observing, not just the rights, but the duties of membership/belonging/participation in a defined group with its own structure, rules, customs, and leaders.

THE GAP

> *Manager:* "Loyalty is dead!"
>
> *Gen Zer:* "It works both ways. You'll keep me working here as long as you need me. If you stop paying me, I will stop coming to work. And vice versa: I'll keep working here as long as it makes sense for me. No hard feelings if I leave. All you have to do is stop paying me and we go our separate ways."

THE BRIDGE: WHAT YOU, THE MANAGER, NEED TO REMEMBER

Is loyalty dead? For many years in our research, we've been asking people of all ages: "Are you loyal to your employer?"

Most would assume that the oldest, most experienced people would probably evince the most employee loyalty, while the youngest, Gen Zers, would be the most disloyal. The conventional wisdom says that employee loyalty has been diminishing steadily from one generation to the next; from the Boomers to Generation X to Generation Y and now to Z. Funny enough, our research shows just the opposite. The older the person, the more likely he is to say, "No." The younger the person, the more likely she is to say "Yes." Not only that, but from X to Y to Z, over the years, younger people in the workplace have become more and more likely to say "Yes." That no longer surprises me. The reason is that the very meaning of employee loyalty is changing.

What today's young people mean when they say they are "loyal" to their employer is the kind of loyalty you get in a marketplace. It's the kind of loyalty you give to a customer: You get exactly as much loyalty as you pay for, and it lasts as long as you keep paying. Of course, it's not just money that Gen Zers are looking for in a job.

No hard feelings to you, the employer. It's just not about you. It's about them. Every step of the way, Gen Zers are going to try to fit their work situation into the life experience they are trying to create for themselves. The thing is that, in the earlier life and career stages, especially in these times, what's going on in their lives at any given moment is not so easy to assess. And it is often a moving target:

- Sometimes new, young workers just want a place to hide out and collect a paycheck. I call that *just a job*.
- Sometimes new, young workers are taking stock and trying to figure out what they really want to do next. I call this a *weigh station job*.
- Sometimes new, young workers look at work as a place to hang out with friends. I call this a *peer group job*.
- Sometimes new, young workers find a job opportunity that aligns with their deep interests and priorities.
- Sometimes new, young workers see a job as an opportunity to work like crazy for a period of time with the chance of a giant payoff.
- Sometimes what a new, young person might value in a job is an unusual opportunity to meet an idiosyncratic need or want. It might be to work a very particular schedule, or work with particular individuals, or work in a particular location, or learn a particular skill, or do a particular task, or engage in some non-work activity (sleeping or reading or watching television) on the job. I call this a *needle-in-a-haystack job*.
- The very best case is what I refer to as a *self-building job*. When new young workers look at the job as a chance to make an impact while building themselves up with your resources. They hope to learn, grow, and collect proof of their ability to add value. As long as you keep supporting their self-building, this will bring out their best for the most sustained period.

This is very frustrating to a lot of employers. Managers often point to this unwillingness among young employees to be willing to make personal sacrifices without a clear quid pro quo, without asking "What's in it for me?" To the ears of many older, more experienced people, this sounds a lot like disloyalty, which is sort of like the opposite of good citizenship. The whole idea of "citizenship" is that it is something more. There is an intangible element—a selfless-ness that goes beyond the transactional relationship.

Here's what I always tell managers: "Let go of the idea that good citizenship has to be completely selfless." Good citizenship does not require selflessness. It's ok if there is a quid pro quo. Employment relationships are transactional by nature. Very few people go to work every day who do not need to make a living. Most people would stop coming to work if you stopped paying them. That does not make them disloyal. You can get a very deep level of true commitment—something more—and still have the essence of the relationship be transactional.

Membership, belonging, and participation come with rights and rewards; that is the quid pro quo. What good citizenship requires is this: When you "join," you are also fully accepting, embracing, and promising to observe the duties, even at considerable personal sacri-fice, that are on the other side of that quid pro quo. That means you have to define those duties in no uncertain terms and make it really clear why they are important.

Over time, the power of belonging comes more and more from accepting, embracing, and observing one's duties than it does from enjoying the rights and rewards of membership. But that's one of those secrets of wisdom that only comes with experience and age. You don't need to tell them about that part just yet.

Teaching/Learning Objective

Help them become better citizens by teaching them to accept, em-brace, and observe the duties of membership/belonging/participa-tion in this job in this organization.

Make Them Aware/Make Them Care

Your script: "Here's why you should care about learning to be a great citizen of this organization. Working here is very valuable. Joining this organization comes with a lot of rewards. But the rewards of membership—the rewards of belonging—also go along with consid-erable duties.

"What good citizenship requires is this: When you 'join' an or-ganization like this one, you must be prepared to accept and em-brace and observe the duties—sometimes at considerable personal sacrifice—that go along with all the rewards.

"Like every workplace, this organization has its own structure, rules, customs, and leadership. What good citizenship means in one organization may be very different from what it means in another.

"What does this mean for you? First, it means you need to know what really matters to you. What is 'in it for you' here in this job? And what is that worth to you? Second, it means you need to understand our structure, rules, customs, and leadership and what that requires of you. You need to really understand what it means to be a good workplace citizen in this organization. Third, you must feel really great about accepting, embracing, and observing the duties of belonging here—what it means to be a good workplace citizen here—along with the rewards.

Good Citizenship: Lesson Plan 1—Introduction

Step One　*Brainstorm:* What does "good citizenship" mean to you?

Step Two　Consider the following definition of "good citizenship": "Accepting, embracing, and observing, not just the rights and rewards, but the duties of membership/belonging/participation in a defined group with its own structure, rules, customs, and leadership."

Brainstorm: Why is this approach to citizenship in the best interests of the organization? Why is this approach to citizenship in your best interests as an employee? Are there good reasons to reject this approach to citizenship?

Step Three　Now consider the rights and rewards of being an employee in this organization.

Brainstorm: What are the rights and rewards that benefit you as an employee here? What does it mean to accept, embrace, and observe those rights and rewards?

Step Four　Consider the other side of the equation.

Brainstorm: What does it mean to be a "good citizen"—as an employee—in this organization? What are your duties as a good citizen? Go beyond just "doing your job." Exactly HOW does a good citizen in this organization go about doing his or her job?

- ◆ Are there formal requirements?
- ◆ Are there informal requirements?
- ◆ What are the parameters among those who are considered "good citizens"?
- ◆ What should be the parameters of "good citizenship" in this organization?

Step Five　Now make a list of the duties of good citizenship as an employee in this organization.

Step Six　Now consider the list of duties, one by one. For each one: Can you think of examples of individuals exemplifying good citizenship by accepting, embracing and observing these duties? What does it mean for you to accept, embrace, and observe those duties?

Step Seven   Now go through the list of duties and define each of the duties with bullet points or short sentences. Define each of the duties of citizenship.

Step Eight   Consider each of the duties of citizenship as defined, one by one. For each one: How are you doing personally when it comes to fulfilling this duty of good citizenship? Are you performing at 100 percent? If not, then what percentage would you give your performance? Where is the gap? What do you need to do to improve?

Good Citizenship: Lesson Plan 2—The "Respect for Others" Model

Step One Consider the following model of "good workplace citizenship."

- Respect for other people's time
- Respect for other people's work space
- Respect for other people's knowledge and experience
- Respect for other people's labor
- Respect for other people's resources
- Respect for other people's ideas and creativity
- Respect for other people's relationships at work
- Respect for other people's well-being

Step Two What do you think of this model?

Brainstorm: Why might this approach to citizenship be in the best interests of the organization? Why might this approach to citizenship be in your best interests as an employee? What happens when "respecting" one of these things is inconsistent with "respecting" another?

Step Three Consider each of the "best practices" or duties in the model above, one by one. For each, answer the following questions: Can you think of examples of individuals exemplifying good citizenship in this way? What would it mean for you? Define each of the "best practices" or duties above with bullet points or short sentences.

Step Four Now once again consider each of the duties in the model above, as you've defined them. For each, answer the following questions:

- How are people in our organization (or team) overall doing when it comes to this approach to good citizenship? What can we do to become better?
- How are you doing as an individual when it comes to this approach? What can you do to be better?

Step Five HOMEWORK. Consider bringing this model forward with you into your day-to-day work. Try to be a better citizen, according to this model. Keep track of how you are doing in writing. Talk about it with your manager in your one-on-ones.

Good Citizenship: Lesson Plan 3—The "Best Interests" Model

Step One   Consider the following model of "good workplace citizenship."

- Do what's best for the mission.
- Do what's best for the company.
- Do what's best for the customers.
- Do what's best for the employees.
- Do what's best for our partners and vendors.
- Do what's best for our community.

Step Two   What do you think of this model?

Brainstorm: Why might this approach to citizenship be in the best interests of the organization? Why might this approach to citizenship be in your best interests as an employee? What happens when "what's best" for one is inconsistent with "what's best" for another?

Step Three   Consider each of the "best practices" or duties in the model above, one by one. For each, answer the following questions: Can you think of examples of individuals exemplifying good citizenship in this way? What would it mean for you? Define each of the "best practices" or duties above with bullet points or short sentences.

Step Four   Now once again consider each of the duties in the model above, as you've defined them. For each, answer the following questions:

- How are people in our organization (or team) overall doing when it comes to this approach to good citizenship? What can we do to get better?
- How are you doing as an individual when it comes to this approach? What can you do to get better?

Step Five   HOMEWORK. Consider bringing this model forward with you into your day-to-day work. Try to be a better citizen, according to this model. Keep track of how you are doing in writing. Talk about it with your manager in your one-on-ones.

Good Citizenship: Lesson Plan 4—The "Civic" Model

Step One   Consider the following model of "good citizenship."

- Deliberating civilly
- Monitoring and reporting on activities of decision makers
- Building coalitions
- Managing conflicts fairly and without violence
- Petitioning, documenting, speaking, and providing evidence and arguments in favor and against different positions

Step Two   What do you think of this model?

Brainstorm: Why might this approach to citizenship be in the best interests of the organization? Why might this approach to citizenship in your best interests as an employee? What are the downsides of this more "civic" way of thinking about citizenship?

Step Three   Consider each of the "best practices" or duties in the model above, one by one. For each, answer the following questions: Can you think of examples of individuals exemplifying good citizenship in this way? What would it mean for you? Define each of the "best practices" or duties above with bullet points or short sentences.

Step Four   Now once again consider each of the duties in the model above, as you've defined them. For each, answer the following questions:

- How are people in our organization (or team) overall doing when it comes to this approach to good citizenship? What can we do to become better?
- How are you doing as an individual when it comes to this approach? What can you do to be better?

Step Five   HOMEWORK. Consider bringing this model forward with you into your day-to-day work. Try to be a better citizen, according to this model. Keep track of how you are doing in writing. Talk about it with your manager in your one-on-ones.

Good Citizenship: Lesson Plan 5—The "Communitarian" Model

Step One   Consider the following model of "good citizenship":

- ◆ Honesty
- ◆ Compassion
- ◆ Respect
- ◆ Responsibility
- ◆ Courage

Step Two   What do you think of this model?

Brainstorm: Why might this approach to citizenship be in the best interests of the organization? Why might this approach to citizenship be in your best interests as an employee? What are the downsides?

Step Three   Consider each of the "best practices" or duties in the model above, one by one. For each, answer the following questions: Can you think of examples of individuals exemplifying good citizenship in this way? What would it mean for you? Define each of the "best practices" or duties above with bullet points or short sentences.

Step Four   Now once again consider each of the duties in the model above, as you've defined them. For each, answer the following questions:

- ◆ How are people in our organization (or team) overall doing when it comes to this approach to good citizenship? What can we do to become better?
- ◆ How are you doing as an individual when it comes to this approach? What can you do to be better?

Step Five   HOMEWORK. Consider bringing this model forward with you into your day-to-day work. Try to be a better citizen, according to this model. Keep track of how you are doing in writing. Talk about it with your manager in your one-on-ones.

Good Citizenship: Lesson Plan 6—The "Common Sense" Model

Step One Consider the following model of "good citizenship."

- Exhibit respect, kindness, courtesy, and good manners.
- Prepare in advance before meetings or one-on-one conversations so you are brief, direct, and clear.
- Never speak of a problem unless you have thought of at least one potential solution.
- Take personal responsibility for everything you say and do.
- Don't make excuses when you make a mistake.
- Don't blame or complain.
- Don't take yourself too seriously.
- Always take your commitments and responsibilities seriously.
- Always give people credit for their achievements, no matter how small.

Step Two What do you think of this model?

Brainstorm: Why might this approach to citizenship be in the best interests of the organization? Why might this approach to citizenship be in your best interests as an employee? What are the downsides?

Step Three Consider each of the "best practices" or duties in the model above, one by one. For each, answer the following questions: Can you think of examples of individuals exemplifying good citizenship in this way? What would it mean for you? Define each of the "best practices" or duties above with bullet points or short sentences.

Step Four Now once again consider each of the duties in the model above, as you've defined them. For each, answer the following questions:

- ◆ How are people in our organization (or team) overall doing when it comes to this approach to good citizenship? What can we do to become better?
- ◆ How are you doing as an individual when it comes to this approach? What can you do to be better?

Step Five HOMEWORK. Consider bringing this model forward with you into your day-to-day work. Try to be a better citizen, according to this model. Keep track of how you are doing in writing. Talk about it with your manager in your one-on-ones.

Good Citizenship: Lesson Plan 7—The "Solid Standards" Model

Step One   Consider the following model of "good citizenship."

"Solid standards":
- Be on time, or a little bit early.
- Don't take long breaks.
- Don't leave early, and even stay a little late sometimes.
- Under-promise and over-deliver.
- Don't bad mouth others, and try not to speak of others unless they are present.
- Keep your word.
- Keep confidences.
- Be an accurate source of information.
- Don't keep other people waiting.
- Overdress, rather than under-dress.
- Practice old-fashioned good manners, that is, saying "please," "thank you," "you're welcome," "excuse me," "I'm sorry," and, if appropriate, addressing people by Mr., Ms., Doctor, Professor, and so on.

Step Two   What do you think of this model?

Brainstorm: Why might this approach to citizenship be in the best interests of the organization? Why might this approach to citizenship be in your best interests as an employee? What are the downsides?

Step Three   Consider each of the "best practices" or duties in the model above, one by one. For each, answer the following questions: Can you think of examples of individuals exemplifying good citizenship in this way? What would it mean for you? Define each of the "best practices" or duties above with bullet points or short sentences.

Step Four   Now once again consider each of the duties in the model above, as you've defined them. For each, answer the following questions:

- How are people in our organization (or team) overall doing when it comes to this approach to good citizenship? What can we do to get better?
- How are you doing as an individual when it comes to this approach? What can you do to get better?

Step Five HOMEWORK. Consider bringing this model forward with you into your day-to-day work. Try to be a better citizen, according to this model. Keep track of how you are doing in writing. Talk about it with your manager in your one-on-ones.

Good Citizenship: Lesson Plan 8—The "Personal Sacrifice" Model

Step One   Consider the following model of "good citizenship."

"Personal sacrifices":
- Giving your employer the benefit of the doubt when explanations are not immediately forthcoming
- Showing patience in the face of protracted difficulties or delayed rewards
- Displaying candor and cooperation with peers and managers
- Offering one's employer first rights of refusal in the face of a seemingly better offer
- Doing more than required and expending discretionary effort in your work
- Arriving early, staying late, working through breaks, coming to work without notice at the last minute, and chipping in to perform additional work outside one's job description in order to cover for someone else coming up short

Step Two   What do you think of this model?

Brainstorm: Why might this approach to citizenship be in the best interests of the organization? Why might this approach to citizenship be in your best interests as an employee? What are the downsides?

Step Three   Consider each of the "best practices" or duties in the model above, one by one. For each, answer the following questions: Can you think of examples of individuals exemplifying good citizenship in this way? What would it mean for you? Define each of the "best practices" or duties above with bullet points or short sentences.

Step Four   Now once again consider each of the duties in the model above, as you've defined them. For each, answer the following questions:

♦ How are people in our organization (or team) overall doing when it comes to this approach to good citizenship? What can we do to get better?

♦ How are you doing as an individual when it comes to this approach? What can you do to get better?

Step Five   HOMEWORK. Consider bringing this model forward with you into your day-to-day work. Try to be a better citizen, according to this model. Keep track of how you are doing in writing. Talk about it with your manager in your one-on-ones.

Good Citizenship: Lesson Plan 9—The Theodore Roosevelt Model

Step One Consider the following very simple model of "good citizenship":

> *Theodore Roosevelt, the twenty-sixth President of the United States, defined good citizenship for an individual as being "able and willing to pull his weight."*

Step Two What do you think of this model?

Brainstorm: Why might this approach to citizenship be in the best interests of the organization? Why might this approach to citizenship be in your best interests as an employee? Are there good reasons to reject this approach to citizenship?

Step Three Consider this model of good citizenship. Can you think of examples of individuals exemplifying good citizenship in this way? What would it mean for you to accept, embrace, and observe this approach to good citizenship?

Step Four Now consider:

- How are people in our organization (or team) overall doing when it comes to this approach to good citizenship? What can we do to get better?
- How are you doing as an individual when it comes to this approach? What can you do to get better?

Step Five
HOMEWORK. Consider bringing this model forward with you into your day-to-day work. Try to be a better citizen, according to this model. Keep track of how you are doing in writing. Talk about it with your manager in your one-on-ones.

Good Citizenship: Lesson Plan 10—Create Your Own Model

Step One Create your own model of "good citizenship."

Step Two Make the case for your model.

Brainstorm: Why might this approach to citizenship be in the best interests of the organization? Why might this approach to citizenship be in your best interests as an employee? What are the downsides?

Step Three Consider each of the "best practices" or duties in the model you create, one by one. For each, answer the following questions: Can you think of examples of individuals exemplifying good citizenship in this way? What would it mean for you? Define each of the "best practices" or duties above with bullet points or short sentences.

Step Four Now once again consider each of the duties in the model above, as you've defined them. For each, answer the following questions:

  ◆ How are people in our organization (or team) overall doing when it comes to this approach to good citizenship? What can we do to get better?
  ◆ How are you doing as an individual when it comes to this approach? What can you do to get better?

Step Five HOMEWORK. Consider bringing this model forward with you into your day to day work. Try to be a better citizen, according to this model. Keep track of how you are doing in writing. Talk about it with your manager in your one-on-ones.

How to Teach Service

Service: Approaching relationships in terms of what you have to offer—respect, commitment, hard work, creativity, sacrifice—rather than what you need or want.

THE GAP

> *Manager:* "You know, I guess what I want to say to them is that Bob Dylan said it best: 'You're gonna have to serve someone.'"
>
> *Gen Zer:* "What about this whole idea of 'servant leadership' I read about? I got the impression that leaders are supposed to serve us, according to that theory. There's a lot of ways to look at it."

THE BRIDGE: WHAT YOU, THE MANAGER, NEED TO REMEMBER

What is so special about the old-fashioned idea of service? On a strictly rational basis, service is just another spin on the transactional logic of employment, like any market-based relationship: you get what you pay for. That notion of "service" is reciprocal, quid pro quo, each side of the value proposition.

Yet, somehow, like citizenship, the concept of service implies more. There is a yearning desire on the part of many older, more experienced people for a demonstration of something deeper—a kind of selflessness. When people talk about the missing values of "service" as a mindset, there is almost a religious or moralistic implication. Somehow, the spirit of generosity and the act of giving are supposed to have their own hidden long-term benefits to the generous giver. Maybe it is just a more cosmic sense of the quid pro quo—like Karma. What goes around comes around.

Whether or not this is true on some cosmic level, it is a very hard case to make to today's young workforce, unless you happen to be their spiritual adviser. Nonetheless, experience does show that when you give people a taste of selfless giving, it can be so nourishing that it creates its own self-reinforcing virtuous cycle. In any case, whatever philosophical or logical underpinning one chooses, this deep sense of "service" for its own sake is in great demand and short supply.

It is easy to understand why this might be a very desirable mindset, especially in one's employees. I remember a senior partner at the law firm where I was an associate in the early 1990s who said to me: "You should be prepared to jump in front of a bus for this firm." I said to myself, "For G-d? Yes. For my family? Yes. For my country? Yes. For this firm? I don't think so."

Ask yourself: If you want to ask your employees to give of themselves with a level of selflessness—service for its own sake—then what exactly are you asking them to serve?

Is it the organization?

The leadership?

You, the manager?

Their co-workers?

The customers?

The mission?

The most obvious answer, especially with the Millennial Generation's reputation for idealism, is "mission." Mission-driven work draws young people in particular who want to serve others by giving of themselves: The military is a common example; serving in the military is dangerous and doesn't pay well, but it gives young people the chance to help keep their country strong and their fellow citizens safe. Charitable work: Feeding the hungry, building houses for the poor. Health care: Healing the sick is definitely mission-driven work! Mission-driven work is instructive precisely because it draws those who are more inclined to feel that "something beyond" motivation that looks like old-fashioned loyalty.

I was struck by this comment from a very experienced leader in a large hospital: "In health care, we have always attracted people based on our healing mission. That's still true today for most of the young people. The healing mission brings them in the door. But as soon as they walk through the door, they want to know how this job compares to other jobs they could find doing the same mission: What's the pay? What are the hours? How are the people? What are the work conditions? In other words: It's the mission, plus, plus, plus."

I've heard this from so many leaders in mission-driven organizations. No matter how committed they may be to the mission, when mission-driven work is also the source of their livelihood, employees usually care a lot about making sure the transactional elements of the job are also fair and square. That's especially true if there are multiple employers for whom the employee might pursue the same or a similar mission. Even in the military (where you can't exactly go work for the competition), you can choose the Army or the Navy or the Air Force or the Marines or the Coast Guard, or you may be able to pursue a similar mission in national security or intelligence work or law enforcement or public safety or rescue or diplomacy or The Peace Corps or whatever. In a free market for labor, even mission-driven employees are usually going to make their career choices based on mission, plus, plus, plus.

Of course, every employer has a mission of one sort of another. Some missions are more charitable than others. If your organization's mission is to sell a middle-price-range casual dining experience, that is a perfectly valid mission well worth pursuing! And I thank you on behalf of all of us who enjoy your meals. But let's agree that this is not exactly a "charitable" mission. No doubt a big part of what the owners are trying to do is make money. Can you blame them? So how can they blame their employees—of any age—for asking: "What's in it for me?"

Remember: If you can introduce them to the concept of service for its own sake and start to give them a taste of selfless giving, this can be such a nourishing experience that it creates its own self-reinforcing virtuous cycle.

Teaching/Learning Objective

Help them develop a service mindset by learning to focus on what they have to offer in any relationship—getting into the habit of giving respect, commitment, hard work, creativity, and sacrifice.

Make Them Aware/Make Them Care

Your script: "Here's why you should care about developing a service mindset.

"Yes, you are getting paid and you reap the rewards and benefits of being an employee in this organization. So, yes, the organization is your customer. The leadership is your customer. Your manager is your customer. The customers are your customers. Your colleagues here are your customers. Even our partners and vendors are your customers. In relation to you, in this job, everyone is your customer. In this scenario, you are the only one who is not the customer.

"But there is much more to the service mindset than the other side of your paycheck! The truth that everybody knows but nobody likes to acknowledge is that one super-high-performing employee is worth more on some deep level—and is valued so much more by everyone—than three or four mediocre employees.

"If you are one of those high-performing employees, you already know that. If you are not one of those high-performing employees, you should learn that and become one! Where do you begin?

"At the very least, you need to know the bare minimum requirements and the gold standard of performance, the cardinal rules of conduct and the outer limits of your discretion. In every working relationship with every person at every level, make sure you understand not only how to meet the basic expectations of the job, but how to go above and beyond those expectations. If you fail to meet a commitment, be honest and forthright about it. If you make a commitment, deliver on that commitment.

"If you don't get the extra rewards you hope for—or deserve—right away, be patient. Be understanding. After all, doing a great job and delivering on your commitments is what you were hired to do in the first place. That's why you are paid and you keep working here. If you don't benefit immediately from bending over backward and jumping through hoops, then write off the short-term loss as a cost of doing business, an investment in the bank account of your reputation at work. Or perhaps a long-term deposit in your karmic 'service' account.

"Build a reputation, not only for doing great work every day, all day long, ahead of schedule, under budget, and with a big smile on your face. Once you deliver on that part of the deal consistently for some period of time, you put yourself in a position to seize opportunities to go above and beyond. When they present themselves, focus on the value you bring to the table: What hard work can you offer? What extra efforts can you make? What value can you add? Look out for really tough assignments, special assignments, and roles that are hard to fill. Look for ways you can sacrifice to save your boss, your colleagues, your direct reports, and anyone and everyone else time, energy, resources, and trouble. Sometimes, the best thing you can do is sacrifice, suffer, and give, give, give, and give until it hurts.

"Don't be annoyed when all the pressure is on you. Instead, be grateful: This is your big chance to prove yourself and make a huge investment in your growing reputation for service."

Service: Lesson Plan 1—Introduction

Step One   *Brainstorm:* What does "service" mean to you?

Step Two   Consider the following definition of "service": "Approaching relationships in terms of what you have to offer—respect, commitment, hard work, creativity, sacrifice—rather than what you need or want."

Brainstorm: Why is this approach to citizenship in the best interests of the organization? Why is this approach to citizenship in your best interests as an employee?

Step Three   Consider the following dimensions of service. For each one: Why is this an important component of service?

- ◆ Offering respect
- ◆ Offering commitment
- ◆ Offering hard work
- ◆ Offering creativity
- ◆ Offering sacrifice

Step Four   Consider the following dimensions of service. For each one: Can you think of examples of individuals exemplifying this dimension? Can you describe the example in detail? What happened? Where? When? Who was involved?

- ◆ Offering respect
- ◆ Offering commitment
- ◆ Offering hard work
- ◆ Offering creativity
- ◆ Offering sacrifice

Step Five   Consider the following dimensions of service. For each one: Can you think of examples of a time when you exemplified this dimension—inside or outside of work? Can you describe the example in detail? What happened? Where? When? Who else was involved?

- Offering respect
- Offering commitment
- Offering hard work
- Offering creativity
- Offering sacrifice

Step Six Now consider the following dimensions of service again. For each one: Define each one with bullet points or short sentences.

- Offering respect
- Offering commitment
- Offering hard work
- Offering creativity
- Offering sacrifice

Step Seven Consider the dimensions of service. For each one: How are you doing personally when it comes to this dimension of service? Are you performing at 100 percent? If not, then what percentage would you give your performance? Where is the gap? What do you need to do to improve?

- Offering respect
- Offering commitment
- Offering hard work
- Offering creativity
- Offering sacrifice

Service: Lesson Plan 2—Common Myths About "Service" in the Workplace

Consider the following myths about the nature of "service" in the workplace, one by one. For each one: Why is this statement a myth? Have you ever seen this myth in action? Can you describe the example in detail? What happened? Where? When? Who was involved? What lessons do you draw from this example?

Myth 1: If you are a high performer, then your boss shouldn't tell you how to do your job.

Myth 2: In order to be creative at work, you need to be left alone to do things your own way.

Myth 3: If someone else is receiving special treatment, then you should, too.

Myth 4: The path to success is catering to your boss's style and preferences.

Myth 5: "Making friends" with your boss is smart workplace politics.

Myth 6: Hiding from mistakes and problems is a good way to avoid trouble.

Myth 7: No news is good news, but being "coached" on your performance is bad news.

Myth 8: If your boss doesn't like to read paperwork, you don't need to keep track of your performance in writing.

Myth 9: If you don't play "politics," then you'll have a hard time getting ahead in the workplace.

Myth 10: Some bosses are just too busy to meet with you.

Service: Lesson Plan 3—Realities About Service in the Workplace

Consider the following realities about the nature of "service" in the workplace, one by one. For each one: Why is this statement a reality? Have you ever seen this reality in action? Can you describe the example in detail? What happened? Where? When? Who was involved? What lessons do you draw from this example?

Reality: No matter how good a person is at a job, everybody needs guidance, direction, and support in order to succeed.

Reality: If you really want to be creative at work, the first thing you need to know is exactly what is and what is not up to you.

Reality: If you want special treatment, you should be prepared to go the extra mile to earn it.

Reality: Your best path to success is making sure you have a regular structured dialogue where you receive the guidance, direction, support, and coaching you need.

Reality: The smartest workplace politics are to keep your work relationships focused on the work.

Reality: When you deal with mistakes and problems as they occur, you are much more likely to solve them while they are still small and manageable, before they get out of control.

Reality: Being coached on your performance is an opportunity to improve—and that is always good news.

Reality: You owe it to yourself and the organization to keep track of everything you do in writing.

Reality: Whether or not you are "political," if you learn and practice the "service" mindset, then you will be everybody's "go to" person.

Reality: No matter how busy your boss may be, your boss does not have time *not* to meet with you on a regular basis.

Service: Lesson Plan 4—Myths Versus Realities in the Workplace

Consider the following myth versus reality pairs, along with the explanations for why for each one. Have you seen examples of this in the real world? Can you describe the example in detail? What happened? Where? When? Who was involved? What lessons do you draw from this example?

> *Myth 1:* If you are a high performer, then your boss shouldn't tell you how to do your job.
>
> versus
>
> *Reality:* No matter how good a person is at a job, everybody needs guidance, direction, and support in order to succeed.

WHY? You need to make sure your work fits with your overall company's mission. You need to have articulated goals and the guidelines and parameters for your tasks and responsibilities spelled out. You need to be given concrete deadlines, clear timelines, and reasonable performance benchmarks to meet. And your boss is the person who must communicate these requirements to you and make sure you stay on track . That's the only way to become and remain a high performer. But if you are a high performer, you probably already know all that.

> *Myth 2:* In order to be creative at work, you need to be left alone to do things your own way.
>
> versus
>
> *Reality:* If you really want to be creative at work, the first thing you need to know is exactly what is and what is not up to you.

WHY? So much of what is done at work is simply not up to you. You need to know the requirements of every task, responsibility, or project before you can even think about being creative. Even if you are in a creative position, only when you know what is actually up to you have you uncovered the small space in which you can be creative.

Myth 3: If someone else is receiving special treatment, then you
   should, too.
   versus
Reality: If you want special treatment, then you have to go the
   extra mile to earn it.

WHY? If someone else is receiving special treatment, then figure
out exactly what that person did to earn the special treatment and
what exactly you need to do to earn the special treatment you want.
Why would it be fair to treat everybody in a workplace exactly the
same? That's only fair in a commune. If your co-workers are receiving
rewards that you are not receiving, take that as a big reality check.
What you need is a fair and accurate assessment of your performance
so that you can continually improve and, thereby, earn more of the
rewards you want. Don't be the squeaky wheel asking for more. Be
the self-starting high performer who is constantly earning more.

Myth 4: The path to success is catering to your boss's style and
   preferences.
   versus
Reality: Your best path to success is making sure you have a
   regular structured dialogue where you receive the guidance,
   direction, support, and coaching you need.

WHY? It is true that you need to align yourself with what
"works" for each of your bosses? Some bosses prefer updates
in writing; others prefer verbal reports. Some bosses prefer big-
picture reports. Others like to keep track of the details. You should
certainly try to tune in to each boss's preferences, but you cannot afford to compromise the basic elements you need in order
to succeed: clear and realistic expectations every step of the way,
the necessary resources to complete your tasks, fair, accurate, and
honest feedback, and appropriate recognition and rewards for
your work.

Myth 5: "Making friends" with your boss is smart workplace
   politics.
   versus

Reality: The smartest workplace politics are to keep your work relationships focused on the work.

WHY? False friendships are a waste of time. Friendships may be wonderful in your personal life, but they are likely to complicate your situation at work. That is not to say that real friendships do not or should not occur in the workplace. Of course they do. Real friendships develop over time at work, including friendships with your boss. If that's your situation, then you'll have to work hard to protect that friendship from the realities of the workplace. What are the best workplace politics? Build authentic relationships with your boss, developing genuine rapport by talking about the work.

Myth 6: Hiding from mistakes and problems is a good way to avoid trouble.
versus
Reality: When you deal with mistakes and problems as they occur, you are much more likely to solve them while they are still small and manageable, before they get out of control.

WHY? When you gloss over small mistakes without solving them, sometimes they drift away, but they are likely to recur. Small problems that recur incessantly cause difficult confrontations when co-workers or the boss finally explodes in an outburst of frustration. Other times, those recurring small problems become part of the fabric of your work. But sometimes small mistakes and problems fester and grow and, over time, become big problems. Solving a problem after it has festered is much more difficult than preventing that problem in the first place or solving it while it is smaller. Plus, in the midst of a problem, neither you nor your boss is going to be at your best. By then, everybody is stressed, frustrated, and in a hurry. If you include regular problem solving in your ongoing one-on-one dialogue with every single boss, then nine out of ten performance problems will be solved quickly and easily or will be avoided altogether.

Myth 7: No news is good news, but being "coached" on your performance is bad news.
versus

Reality: Being coached on your performance is an opportunity to improve—and that is always good news.

WHY? Good coaching is the constant banter of focus, improvement, and accountability: "What can I teach you right now? What can you improve right now?" A great coach helps you remember to be purposeful about every single detail to build your skills. From focusing, you learn focus itself. Look for the real teachers among your bosses and soak up their teachings. Assure the boss that you very much welcome candid feedback in detail, both positive and corrective. Try to turn every one-on-one conversation with your boss into a coaching session.

Myth 8: If your boss doesn't like to read paperwork, you don't need to keep track of your performance in writing.
    versus
Reality: You owe it to yourself and the organization to keep track of everything you do in writing.

WHY? Most managers monitor employee performance only incidentally, when they happen to observe the employee working; when they are presented with the employee's work product; if there is a big win; or if there is a notable problem. They rarely document employee performance unless they are required to do so, leaving no written track record other than those bottom-line reports that tell so little about the day-to-day actions of each employee. Whether or not your boss keeps track of your day-to-day performance in writing, you should.

Myth 9: If you are not "political," then you'll have a hard time getting ahead in the workplace.
    versus
Reality: Whether or not you "play politics," learn and practice the "service" mindset; then you will be everybody's "go to" person.

WHY? Some people are unusually charismatic, observant, receptive, quick-witted, articulate, engaging, energetic, and likeable. That does not help him or her anywhere near as much as being the person who is always focused on the work product he or she has to offer.

Myth 10: Some bosses are just too busy to meet with you.
     versus
Reality: No matter how busy your boss may be, your boss does not have time *not* to meet with you on a regular basis.

WHY? When your boss doesn't spend time one-on-one with you, things go wrong—sometimes very wrong. That's because expectations often remain unclear, misunderstandings occur, you don't obtain the resources you need, you don't receive regular feedback to guide you, and even if you succeed against all odds, you probably won't receive the credit you deserve. If you push your boss to put the management time where it belongs—up front before anything goes right, wrong, or average—things will go much better. If you make sure the time every boss spends with you is effective and pays off in productivity, bosses are going to want to give you that time. You will gain a reputation for making good use of management time.

Service: Lesson Plan 5—The "Be a Great Employee" Model of Service

Step One   Consider the following vision of the service mindset in the workplace:

Be the employee who says to every boss, "Great news, I'm going to make a commitment to serve! I'm going to help you by doing a lot of work very well, very fast, all day long. I'm going to work with you to make sure I understand exactly what you expect of me. On every task, I'm going to break big deadlines into smaller, concrete performance benchmarks. I'm going to learn standard operating procedures and use checklists. I'm going to keep track of everything I'm doing and exactly how I'm doing it. I'm going to help you monitor, measure, and document my performance every step of the way. I'm going to solve problems as soon as they occur and, if I come to you for your help, you'll know I really need you. I'm going to learn and grow and be able to take on more and more responsibility. Count on me. With your help, I'm going to be really valuable to you!"

Step Two   *Brainstorm:* Can you think of examples of individuals exemplifying this service mindset? Can you describe the example in detail? What happened? Where? When? Who was involved?

Step Three   *Brainstorm:* Can you think of examples of a time when you exemplified this approach? Can you describe the example in detail? What happened? Where? When? Who else was involved?

Step Four   *Brainstorm:* How are you doing personally when it comes to this dimension of service? Are you performing at 100 percent? If not, then what percentage would you give your performance? Where is the gap? What do you need to do to improve?

Service: Lesson Plan 6—The "Service" Approach to One-on-Ones Between Managers and Direct Reports

Step One   *Consider:* The key to figuring out what your manager needs from you is to build a regular one-on-one dialogue with every manager to whom you report.

Brainstorm: What would it look like for you to do that? How many managers do you report to now? Who are they? Consider each of them, one by one. For each one, ask yourself: How often should I meet with this manager? When would be the best time to meet? Where? How long? What should I discuss? How can I prepare? What would it take to start scheduling those one-on-ones on a regular basis?

Step Two   Following is a list of the "four basics" that every person must receive from his or her manager in order to be able to succeed. Consider each of the managers to whom you report, one by one. For each one: Do you receive all four of the basics on a regular basis? Where is the gap? What would it take to improve? What can you do to improve the situation?

The four basics that you absolutely must take responsibility for obtaining in your ongoing dialogue with your boss:

1. Clearly spelled out and reasonable expectations, including specific guidelines and a concrete timetable.
2. The skills, tools, and resources necessary to meet those expectations or else an acknowledgement that you are being asked to meet those expectations without them.
3. Accurate and honest feedback about your performance as well as course-correcting direction when necessary.
4. The fair quid pro quo—recognition and rewards—in exchange for your performance.

Step Three   *Consider:* How often you should meet with your boss or bosses depends partly on the nature of the work you are doing for each of them. How often you should meet with a particular manager will also be determined by his or her particular style and preferences and also by what works for you. In an ideal world, maybe YOU would talk with every single boss—reviewing your work and getting set up for success that day—every single day.

Brainstorm: How are people in our organization (or team) overall doing when it comes to this approach? What can we do to get better?

How are you doing as an individual when it comes to this approach? What can you do to get better?

For each of your managers: How often do you need to meet? Where is the gap? What would it take to improve? What can you do to improve the situation?

Step Four   *Consider:* With each boss, you will have to decide what to focus on and discuss at each one-on-one. Before your meetings, you should ask yourself the following: Are there problems that haven't been spotted yet? Problems that need to be solved? Resources that have to be obtained? Are there any instructions or goals that are not clear? Has anything happened since you last talked that the boss should know about? Are there questions that should be answered by your boss? At the very least, in these one-one-ones, you have to receive updates on your progress. Get input from your boss while you have the chance. And think about what input you should be providing to your boss based on what you are learning on the front line. Strategize together. Try to get a little advice, support, motivation, and, yes, even inspiration once in a while.

Brainstorm: How are people in our organization (or team) overall doing when it comes to this approach? What can we do to get better? How are you doing as an individual when it comes to this approach? What can you do to get better?

For each of your managers: What do you need to be discussing? Where is the gap? What would it take to improve? What can you do to improve the situation?

Step Five   HOMEWORK. Take the initiative. Schedule regular one-on-one meetings with every single manager to whom you report. Make your one-on-one time with every boss brief, straightforward, efficient, and all about the work. But make sure you have that regular one-on-one time with every boss you answer to directly at any given time. Be sure to obtain the four basics listed above.

Service: Lesson Plan 7—The Service Approach to Meeting Attendance and Participation

Step One   Consider the following vision of the service approach to your attendance and participation in meetings:

◆ Meetings serve their purpose. They are ideal for sharing information with the whole group and are often necessary to bring people who working interdependently together to hear about what everyone is doing, what issues are coming up in their projects, and so on. Inevitably, you will attend more than your share of team meetings. How can you make the most of them?

◆ Before attending any meeting or presentation, make sure you know what the meeting is about and whether your attendance is required or requested.

◆ Identify what your role in the meeting is: What information are you responsible for communicating or gathering? Prepare in advance: Is there any material you should review or read before the meeting? Are there any conversations you need to have before the meeting? If you are making a presentation, prepare even more.

◆ Ask yourself exactly what value you have to offer the group. If you are not a primary actor in the meeting, often the best thing you can do is say as little as possible and practice good meeting manners. If you are tempted to speak up, ask yourself: Is this a point that everyone needs to hear, right here and now? If you have a question, could it be asked at a later time, off-line? Remember that some meetings are a waste of time. In those meetings, try not to say a single word that will unnecessarily lengthen it.

Step Two   *Brainstorm:*

◆ How are people in our organization (or team) overall doing when it comes to this approach? What can we do to become better?

- ◆ Can you think of examples of individuals exemplifying this? Can you describe the example in detail? What happened? Where? When? Who was involved?
- ◆ Can you think of examples of a time when you exemplified this? Can you describe the example in detail? What happened? Where? When? Who else was involved?
- ◆ How are you doing as an individual when it comes to this approach? What can you do to get better?

Service: Lesson Plan 8—Helping Your Boss Monitor Your Performance

Step One   Consider the following best practices for helping your boss monitor your performance:

- *Provide drafts or samples of your work in progress on a regular basis.*
- *Seize opportunities to help your boss spot-check your work to identify and solve any hidden problems*
- *Ask your boss to watch you work.* If you want to make absolutely sure that you are accomplishing a task the way your boss wants you to do it, watching you complete a task will give her a clear view of what you are doing and how you are doing it.
- *Give your boss an account of your performance.*
- *Use self-monitoring tools.* Help your boss keep track of your concrete actions by making good, rigorous use of self-monitoring tools like project plans, checklists, and activity logs.
- *Spread the word.* Ask customers, vendors, co-workers, and everyone else you work with to give you honest feedback about your performance in relation to them. Ask them, in writing, "How am I doing?"

Step Two   Take the best practices one at a time.
Brainstorm. For each one:

- How are people in our organization (or team) overall doing when it comes to this approach? What can we do to get better?
- Can you think of examples of individuals exemplifying this? Can you describe the example in detail? What happened? Where? When? Who was involved?
- Can you think of examples of a time when you exemplified this? Can you describe the example in detail? What happened? Where? When? Who else was involved?
- How are you doing as an individual when it comes to this approach? What can you do to get better?

Service: Lesson Plan 9—Putting Yourself on a Performance Improvement Plan

Step One   Consider the following:

> *Put yourself on a PIP—Performance Improvement Plan. In many organizations, PIPs have a bad name. So call it something else if you like. How about a "Continuous Improvement Plan"? Whatever you call it, this is the perfect format for helping your boss document your performance every step of the way: Together with your boss, spell out expectations for your performance in terms of concrete actions that you can control. Keep track in writing as you complete each to-do item and meet each requirement, as you achieve each goal and beat each deadline. Regularly report to your boss exactly how and when your concrete actions met or exceeded the expectations you set together. Help your boss document exactly how and when your concrete actions meet expectations every step of the way.*

Step Two   *Brainstorm:*

- ◆ What do you think about this approach?
- ◆ What would be the benefits to you? What about to your boss? What about to the organization?
- ◆ What would be the burdens?

How to Teach Teamwork

Teamwork: Playing whatever role is needed to support the larger mission; coordinating, cooperating, and collaborating with others in pursuit of a shared goal; supporting and celebrating the success of others.

THE GAP

> *Manager:* "There are too many conflicts on the team: This one doesn't want to work with that one. They form little groups and then stick tight with their little groups, unless there is a falling out. Every one of them wants to be the leader or else the MVP."

> *Gen Zer:* "It just sucks that we don't get to choose who is on our team or how we are going to function as a team. It's all determined for us, and we just have to accept it."

THE BRIDGE: WHAT YOU, THE MANAGER, NEED TO REMEMBER

It should be no surprise that peer relationships are extremely important to Gen Zers. After all, they are the social media generation. Their entire lives, they've been plugged into a virtual peer network and mediate much of their experience through these hand-held mirrors of interactivity.

Does that mean that employers should be scrambling to leverage social media to try to develop Gen Z team connections? Yes . . . but be very careful. The best way to create positive employer branding social media is to have lots of very "loyal" young employees. That's your social media strategy in a nutshell. But it's nearly impossible to reverse engineer the process. Social media is far too diffuse and rapidly evolving to artificially manipulate those organic discussions—especially the viral type that spread out among networks of networks of networks in the organic peer ecosystem of social media.

Many of our clients have been experimenting with other strategies to leverage Gen Zers' strong inclination toward peer networking and peer bonding. Some employers have tried to facilitate peer bonding by creating so-called "self-managed teams." It turns out there is no such thing as a "self-managed team"; somebody always takes charge, sometimes the right person and sometimes a ring leader who causes trouble.

Other organizations have tried to implement "best friend at work" programs, where they try to help employees form friendships with colleagues. Most young people either shrug or cringe at these "best friend" programs.

Some organizations encourage employees to form affinity groups around shared interests, activities, or even causes. These tend to be more or less harmless, unless they become a way to affirm cliques; usually, they are only slight distractions at work, although distractions nonetheless.

Some organizations promote socializing among colleagues through meals, happy hours, events, and parties. Most people of any age can appreciate employer-sponsored events or meals or beverages, unless they become another way to affirm cliques or lead to selective exclusion. After work socializing inevitably excludes those who just want to go home after work . . . or to the gym . . . or to walk the dog . . . or whatever. And often those young employees who appreciate the after-work partying the most find themselves embarrassed in front of their colleagues (and sometimes even on their way out of a job) as a result of some major "social" misstep.

As with social media, it is usually a mistake when employers try too hard to artificially co-opt Gen Zers' peer-bonding inclinations. For one thing, there are many pitfalls to avoid, some noted above. More to the point, it usually just doesn't work.

Our research shows consistently that Gen Zers are least likely to form significant lasting peer bonds in workplaces with less challenging work, less structure, less supervision, and less interaction with authority figures. The greater the challenge, structure, supervision, and interaction with authority figures, the more likely Gen Zers are to form significant peer bonds in the workplace. Yes, the key to creating those so-important authentic personal "loyalties" among your Gen Z employees—like the personal loyalty we see among young people working together in the military—is creating conditions in which they can do lots of challenging work together under the strong direction of a highly engaged leader.

When young soldiers, airmen, marines, and sailors talk about their "loyalty," they invoke first and foremost their commitment to each other—to their peers and to their most immediate leaders. But those peer bonds are hardly forming organically. They are not "self-managed," but rather have a strict chain of command with clear leaders who are strong and highly engaged. They don't choose who is going to be on their team. They don't get to choose their own peer leaders. They don't get to choose their own missions. They don't get to choose their own positions on the team. Not everybody gets to be the MVP. Not everybody gets a trophy. The peer bonding is not forced, but all of the conditions are forced—and the peer bonding follows.

Of course, the military has a rare combination of profound patriotic mission, life-threatening gravity, and extraordinary resources. Those are hard conditions to approximate for most leaders in most workplaces. Still, you can be very thankful if, in your workplace, lives are not on the line. You can still draw many great lessons about building the conditions to support great teamwork: the strongest peer relationships among young people in the workplace (and people of all ages) form in environments with a strong focus on the shared mission, the shared work, and the common ground. Yes, it is important to value and leverage everybody's different strengths on a team. But the key to supporting the spirit of "teamwork," per se, is focusing on what everybody has in common: Nobody on the team chose the team or the mission or the positions or the leaders. But all those on the team did choose to be in this job at this time. As long as they remain here, they are in this together. They must depend on each other in order to succeed. So they must depend on each other and be seen as dependable.

Yes, your best employees can see that they pull more weight than the weaker members of the team. Sometimes they have to be reminded that, no matter how much weight they carry on their own, they are not doing their jobs 100 percent unless they are also helping their other team members succeed.

TEACHING/LEARNING OBJECTIVE

Help them become better "team players" by learning to play whatever role is needed to support the larger mission; coordinating, cooperating, and collaborating with others in pursuit of a shared goal; supporting and celebrating the success of others.

MAKE THEM AWARE/MAKE THEM CARE

Your script: "Here's why you should care about teamwork. No matter where you work, no matter what you do, your work probably involves dealing with other people—internally and externally—here, there, and everywhere. Most likely you are forced to rely on the support and cooperation of many other people in the course of doing your own work every day. That means navigating a lot of interpersonal dynamics and a lot of dependency and interdependency. That's what a lot of people call 'teamwork.'

"You've heard over and over again about the importance of good teamwork at work. Right? For the most part, at work, you don't get to choose who is going to be on your team. You don't get to choose your own leaders. You don't get to choose your own mission. You don't get to choose your own position. Not everybody gets to be the MVP. Not everybody gets a trophy. But everybody on the team did choose to be in this job at this time. As long as you remain here, we are all in this together. We must depend on each other in order to succeed. So we must depend on one another.

"Yes, some people pull more weight than others. Some people do more work, better, faster, and with a better attitude. But don't ever tell yourself you are doing a great job if you are not also being a great team player. Being a great team player is part of your job here. That means staying focused on our shared mission and how each person contributes to that shared mission. It means making yourself available and easy to work with. It means coordinating, cooperating, and collaborating with others. It means playing your assigned position as needed to support the larger effort. It means focusing on the best interest of the whole, sometimes at the expense of your own prominence. It means supporting your other team members and helping them succeed and celebrating their successes.

"Here's the bottom line: Some people really get things done. Right? And there are plenty of times when you need to get things done and you need someone's help. Right? So you want to be able to go to the right people, the ones who really get things done. Those people are known as 'go to' people. That's because everybody— just as you do—wants to 'go to' those people. Get it? 'Go to' people don't just get things done. They get things done for other people. That's why 'go to' people are the most in-demand people in the workplace—because everyone knows they can be relied on to deliver for the team. Be one!"

Teamwork: Lesson Plan 1—Introduction

Step One *Brainstorm:* What does "teamwork" mean to you?

Step Two Consider the following definition of "teamwork": "Playing whatever role is needed to support the larger mission; coordinating, cooperating, and collaborating with others in pursuit of a shared goal; supporting and celebrating the success of others."

Brainstorm: Why is this approach to teamwork in the best interests of the organization? Why is this approach to teamwork in your best interests as an employee?

Step Three Consider the following dimensions of teamwork. For each one: Why is this an important component of teamwork? Teamwork:

- Playing whatever role is needed to support the larger mission
- Coordinating with others in pursuit of a shared goal
- Cooperating with others in pursuit of a shared goal
- Collaborating with others in pursuit of a shared goal
- Supporting the success of others
- Celebrating the success of others

Step Four Consider the following dimensions of teamwork. For each one: Can you think of examples of individuals—inside or outside of work—exemplifying this dimension? Can you describe the example in detail? What happened? Where? When? Who was involved?

Teamwork
- Playing whatever role is needed to support the larger mission
- Coordinating with others in pursuit of a shared goal
- Cooperating with others in pursuit of a shared goal
- Collaborating with others in pursuit of a shared goal
- Supporting the success of others
- Celebrating the success of others

Step Five Consider the following dimensions of teamwork. For each one: Can you think of examples of a time when you exemplified this dimension—inside or outside of work? Can you describe the example in detail? What happened? Where? When? Who else was involved?

Teamwork

- Playing whatever role is needed to support the larger mission
- Coordinating with others in pursuit of a shared goal
- Cooperating with others in pursuit of a shared goal
- Collaborating with others in pursuit of a shared goal
- Supporting the success of others
- Celebrating the success of others

Teamwork: Lesson Plan 2—Defining the Dimensions of Teamwork

Step One   Consider the following dimensions of teamwork. For each one: Define each one. Break it down and spell it out with bullet points or short sentences.

Teamwork
- Playing whatever role is needed to support the larger mission
- Coordinating with others in pursuit of a shared goal
- Cooperating with others in pursuit of a shared goal
- Collaborating with others in pursuit of a shared goal
- Supporting the success of others
- Celebrating the success of others

Step Two   Consider the following dimensions of teamwork. For each one: How are people in our organization (or team) overall doing when it comes to this approach? What can we do to get better?

Teamwork
- Playing whatever role is needed to support the larger mission
- Coordinating with others in pursuit of a shared goal
- Cooperating with others in pursuit of a shared goal
- Collaborating with others in pursuit of a shared goal
- Supporting the success of others
- Celebrating the success of others

Step Three   Consider the following dimensions of teamwork. For each one: How are you doing personally when it comes to this dimension of service? Are you performing at 100 percent? If not, then what percentage would you give your performance? Where is the gap? What do you need to do to improve?

Teamwork
- Playing whatever role is needed to support the larger mission
- Coordinating with others in pursuit of a shared goal

- Cooperating with others in pursuit of a shared goal
- Collaborating with others in pursuit of a shared goal
- Supporting the success of others
- Celebrating the success of others

Teamwork: Lesson Plan 3—Your Role in Relation to the Mission

Step One   Consider the first dimension of being a great team player: Playing whatever role is needed to support the larger mission.
   Brainstorm:

- How would you describe the larger mission of this organization?
- How would you describe your role in relation to the mission?

Step Two   Drill down on your role. Make a list of all the different tasks, responsibilities, and projects that comprise your role. Now take them one by one. For each one: What do you actually do? How exactly does your work on that task, responsibility, or project contribute to the larger mission? Who relies on you to do this work? What are the consequences if you don't deliver? What is the value added when you deliver successfully? How are you doing on this particular contribution to the mission? How can you improve?

Step Three   HOMEWORK. Discuss what you learned from this exercise with your manager in your next one-on-one.

Teamwork: Lesson Plan 4—Coordinating, Cooperating, and Collaborating with Others

Step One   Consider the following dimensions of being a great team player:

- ◆ Coordinating with others in pursuit of a shared goal
- ◆ Cooperating with others in pursuit of a shared goal
- ◆ Collaborating with others in pursuit of a shared goal

Make a list of all the other people at work with whom you must coordinate, cooperate, and collaborate.

Step Two   Consider each of the people on your list, one by one. For each one:

- ◆ How would you describe that person's role in relation to the mission?
- ◆ For what do you need to rely on that person at work?
- ◆ On what work specifically do you coordinate, cooperate, and collaborate?
  - • Where?
  - • When?
  - • How?
  - • Who else is involved?
  - • What happens?
- ◆ How do you need this person to improve? What do you need this person to change so that you can get more of what you need/want?

Step Three   Consider each of the people on your list, again, one by one. For each one:

- ◆ How would you describe that person's role in relation to the mission?
- ◆ For what does that person need to rely on you at work?

- ◆ On what work specifically do you coordinate, cooperate, and collaborate?
  - Where?
  - When?
  - How?
  - Who else is involved?
  - What happens?
- ◆ How do you need to improve? What do you need to change so this person can get more from you?

Step Four   HOMEWORK. Discuss what you learned from this exercise with your manager in your next one-on-one.

Teamwork: Lesson Plan 5—Supporting and Celebrating the Success of Others

Step One   Consider the following dimensions of being a great team player:

- ◆ Supporting the success of others
- ◆ Celebrating the success of others

Make a list of all the people who should be supporting and celebrating your success at work. Presumably, they are also people whose success you should be supporting and celebrating as well.

Step Two   Consider each of the people on your list, one by one. For each one:

- ◆ What does this person do to support your success? Can you think of examples?
- ◆ What does this person do to celebrate your success? Can you think of examples?

Step Three   Consider each of the people on your list, again, one by one. For each one:

- ◆ How would you describe that person's role in relation to the mission?
- ◆ What does success look like for this person in his or her role?
- ◆ What do you currently do to support this person's success?
- ◆ What else can you do? How can you improve?
- ◆ What do you currently do to celebrate this person's success?
- ◆ What else can you do? How can you improve?

Step Four   HOMEWORK. Discuss what you learned from this exercise with your manager in your next one-on-one.

Teamwork: Lesson Plan 6—Identifying Your "Go To" People and Building Relationships with Them

Step One What would it look like for you to actively develop "go-to" people in all the key areas where you have recurring interdependency needs. "Go-to" people are the people you know you can "go to" when you need something. They are people you can rely on. They are responsive. They are effective. They get things done.
Brainstorm:

- How can you identify "go to" people in all the right places?
- What cooperation and assistance do you anticipate needing from other colleagues—internal and external—to do your projects, tasks, and responsibilities?
- Exactly who should you ask for what, when, and how?
- What is the precise nature of the working relationship with each person upon whom you may need to rely?
- What level of cooperation and assistance is appropriate and reasonable to request?
- In each case, is there more than one person to whom you could turn for cooperation and assistance?
- What do you need to do to develop strong mutually supportive working relationships with these "go to" people?

Step Two HOMEWORK. Discuss what you learned from this exercise with your manager in your next one-on-one.

Teamwork: Lesson Plan 7—Becoming a "Go To" Person for Others

Step One   What would it look like for you to become a "go-to" person yourself?

Brainstorm:

- ◆ How can you bend over backward to do things for other people?
- ◆ How can you become super-reliable?
- ◆ How can you become super-responsive?
- ◆ How can you become super-effective in getting things done?
- ◆ How can you make sure you always deliver on your commitments very well, very fast, all day long—especially for known "go-to" people?
- ◆ How can you make sure to conduct yourself always in a professional manner with a great attitude?
- ◆ How can you develop a reputation as a "go-to" person?

Step Two   *Brainstorm:* Can you think of examples of individuals exemplifying the "go-to" person? Can you describe the example in detail? What happened? Where? When? Who was involved?

Step Three   *Brainstorm:* Can you think of examples of a time when you exemplified the "go-to" person? Can you describe the example in detail? What happened? Where? When? Who else was involved?

Step Four   *Brainstorm:* How are you doing personally when it comes to becoming a "go-to" person? Are you performing at 100 percent? If not, then what percentage would you give your performance? Where is the gap? What do you need to do to improve?

Step Five   HOMEWORK. Discuss what you learned from this exercise with your manager in your next one-on-one.

Teamwork: Lesson Plan 8—Using Influence to Get Things Done

Step One Consider how you can become better at gaining greater co-ordination, cooperation, and collaboration from others. Consider your options when it comes to the following strategies for using influence:

- *Build and draw on interpersonal influence.* Conduct yourself always in a businesslike, professional manner. Be the person other people do not want to disappoint.
- *Use the influence of specific commitments.* Clear timelines for deliverables with reminders along the way are more likely to be fulfilled.
- *Seek to influence through persuasion.* Use good reasons to convince other people to deliver: "This is why you should do this for me. This is why it's a good thing for your team, and your company. This is why you should put my request first. This is why nothing else should get in the way."
- *Influence through facilitation.* Do everything possible to help support and assist other people in the fulfillment of their part. What are all the things you can do to make it easier for other people to deliver?

Step Two Consider the strategies above, one by one. For each one: Have you seen examples of this in the real world? Can you describe the example in detail? What happened? Where? When? Who was involved? What lessons can you draw from this example?

Step Three Consider the strategies above, one by one. For each one: How are you doing personally when it comes to using these strategies? Are you performing at 100 percent? If not, then what percentage would you give your performance? Where is the gap? What do you need to do to improve?

Step Four HOMEWORK. Discuss what you learned from this exercise with your manager in your next one-on-one

Teamwork: Lesson Plan 9—Consider the Lessons About Teamwork from This U.S. Air Force Special Operations Team

Step One   Consider the following story exemplifying great teamwork:

> *The young airman, one crew member among the thirteen-member crew of an important military aircraft, describes his role on the team's regular missions (which last as long as ten hours): "My job is to lay face down in a window facing the ground in order to provide visual confirmation of the aircraft's electronic surveillance of the ground below. Basically, I just lie down there with my eyes wide open and focused. We have very advanced systems on the plane, but I am the eyeballs. I need to provide visual [confirmation] to make sure we don't fire on any [friendly forces] or civilians. But I also am watching for muzzle flares which might indicate enemy forces. I also look for enemy fire directed at the plane. When we are fired on, we only have a few seconds to detect that and take countermeasures to protect the plane."*
>
> *For hours at a time, this young Airman stays focused and blinks as little as possible. During a ten-hour mission, there might only be a handful of incidents for which the Airman would actually need to take notice and take action. Asked if it is hard to stay alert on the job, he says: "I don't have a choice. The difference between me giving 99 percent or 110 percent could be the difference between life or death for me, for people on the ground, and for my crew."*
>
> *The crew numbered thirteen. Each person played a narrow, focused role and was critical to the safety and effective operation of the airplane and its mission. And every single one of them knew that they had no choice but to give 110 percent all the time, because the work of every single role is a life-or-death matter. For your sake, I hope that every move you make at work is not a life-or-death matter. Still, if you want to succeed, you would do well to follow this example of teamwork.*

Step Two   *Brainstorm:*

- How would you describe this example of teamwork?
- What is admirable about this approach?
- What can we learn from this story?
- How are people in our organization (or team) overall doing when it comes to this level of teamwork? What can we do to get better?
- How are you doing as an individual when it comes to this approach? What can you do to be better?

About the Author

Bruce Tulgan is an adviser to business leaders all over the world and a sought-after keynote speaker and seminar leader. He is the founder and CEO of RainmakerThinking, Inc., a management research and training firm, as well as RainmakerThinking.training, an online training company. Bruce is the author of numerous books, including the best-selling *It's Okay to Be the Boss* (2007), the classic *Managing Generation X* (1995), *Not Everyone Gets a Trophy* (2009), *It's Okay to Manage Your Boss* (2010), *FAST Feedback* (1999), and his most recent book, *The 27 Challenges Managers Face* (2014). His work has been the subject of thousands of news stories around the world. He has written pieces for numerous publications, including *The New York Times, USA Today, Harvard Business Review, Training* magazine, and *Human Resources*. Bruce also holds a fifth-degree black belt in classical Okinawan Uechi Ryu karate. He lives in New Haven, Connecticut, with his wife Dr. Debby Applegate, author of the Pulitzer-Prize winning biography *The Most Famous Man in America: The Biography of Henry Ward Beecher* (2006), as well as *Madam; The Notorious Life and Times of Polly Adler* (forthcoming). Bruce can be reached by e-mail at brucet@rainmakerthinking.com or you can follow him on Twitter @brucetulgan..

Index